Publisher and Creative Director: Nick Wells
Project Editor: Cat Emslie
Picture Research and Editing: Toria Lyle
Art Director: Mike Spender
Layout Design: Vanessa Green
Digital Design and Production: Chris Herbert
Indexer: Helen Snaith

Special thanks to: Liz Keevill and Rosalind Ormiston for their invaluable contributions; Claire Walker

11

3 5 7 9 10 8 6 4

This edition first published 2007 by
FLAME TREE PUBLISHING
Crabtree Hall, Crabtree Lane
Fulham, London SW6 6TY
United Kingdom

www.flametreepublishing.com

Flame Tree is part of the Foundry Creative Media Co. Ltd

© 2007 The Foundry Creative Media Co. Ltd

ISBN 978-1-84451-870-8

A CIP record for this book is available from the British Library upon request.

Printed in China

Angels

ARTISTS & INSPIRATIONS

Iain Zaczek

FLAME TREE
PUBLISHING

Contents

Introduction 6

Angels and Religion 10

Early Prototypes and Old Testament Angels 12

Archangel Gabriel and the Annunciation 32

Nativity, Madonna and Child 52

Coronation and Assumption of the Virgin 62

Crucifixion and Resurrection 72

Archangel Michael 86

Devils and Rebel Angels 92

Heaven and Judgement 98

Saints and Angels...110

Angelic Interpretations: Classical to Allegorical 118

Guardian Angels...120

Victorian Angels...126

The Music of Angels 136

Cherubim to Cherubs 152

Cupid and Classical Figures 156

Allegorical Figures 186

Credits...198

Index 199

INTRODUCTION

Angels are amongst the best loved and most familiar Christian symbols. For many they evoke childhood memories of Christmas cards, Nativity plays and tree decorations. These heavenly beings have a long pedigree, however, and their image has evolved considerably over the centuries.

Angels act as intermediaries between God and humanity. In the Bible, they serve as divine messengers (their name comes from *angelos*, the Greek word for 'messenger'), though they also have many other duties. They are healers and protectors; they wage war against the devil; and they are celestial courtiers, worshipping around God's throne.

The Old Testament also offered some clues about their appearance. Angels and archangels, it seemed, were male and wingless, virtually indistinguishable from normal men. However, both the seraphim and cherubim did have wings. A typical description can be found in Isaiah: 'Above it stood the seraphims; each one had six wings; with twain he covered his face, and with twain he covered his feet, and with twain he did fly' (Isaiah 6:2).

The Scriptures also made it clear that angels came in many different forms. Only two of these had direct dealings with humans – angels and archangels – though there were several other types. Cherubim and seraphim are familiar terms, but Saint Paul (died *c.* 64 AD) extended the list to nine. These were eventually codified into a workable system by a Syrian monk, known as Dionysius the Pseudo-Areopagite (*fl.* fifth century). In his treatise, *On the Celestial Hierarchies*, he identified nine separate ranks or choirs of angels, which he divided into three hierarchies. The most important of these were the counsellors (seraphim, cherubim and thrones), who remained closest to God. Below them came the governors (powers, dominions and virtues), who controlled the stars and the elements, and finally the messengers (principalities, archangels and angels).

For over a thousand years, this classification of angels was generally accepted, although it did nothing to curb speculation about other aspects of their nature. Were they pure spirit or physical matter? Could they eat or drink? What did angelic speech sound like? And, most famously, how many angels can dance upon the head of a pin? Philosophers came up with answers for many of these questions. Thomas Aquinas (c. 1225–74), for example, believed that angels were essentially incorporeal, and that their visible forms were made up of condensed, shaped and coloured air.

This type of hypothesis was less than helpful to the artists, who were called upon to portray angels in their holy scenes. The earliest examples, dating back to the era of the Roman Catacombs (third century), showed them as wingless males. However, this often made it difficult to identify both the angel and the subject, so alternatives were sought. Artists looked at the guardian spirits and divine messengers from other cultures. They found their main prototypes in the winged creatures from Mesopotamia, dimly remembered from the ancient periods of exile, and from the various winged figures found in classical sculpture.

The conventional image of angels evolved from a combination of these sources, although some questions remained unanswered. How old should angels look? The use of adult classical figures, such as Victory or Fame, as

well as childlike figures, such as Cupid, made this unclear. What should they wear? The robes of many angels had a vaguely classical appearance, but some painters felt uncomfortable with this, believing that it looked too pagan. So, particularly in northern Europe, some angels were attired in modified versions of ecclesiastical dress.

In the end, artists used these uncertainties to their advantage. Angels can appear as adults, when they are battling the rebel angels, but can resemble cheery infants, when they frolic around the Virgin and Child. Increasingly, painters also endowed them with human emotions. They could weep at the Crucifixion, dance for joy at the Nativity or look bemused as they struggled to play a musical instrument.

The value of angels was questioned again in the sixteenth century, when Protestant reformers poured scorn on the notion of celestial choirs, and were deeply suspicious of the veneration shown to named archangels, like Michael and Gabriel. However, they remained ambivalent about the idea of guardian angels and spiritual messengers. So, when the Catholic Church launched its counter-attack, angels were in the vanguard. Rosy-cheeked cherubs swarmed around every scene, and the angelic encounters portrayed by Bernini and El Greco displayed a heightened sense of emotionalism.

In time, this trend became debased. Cherubs became indistinguishable from cupids. Even the famous statue known as *Eros* is actually meant to be an *Angel of Christian Charity*. Even so, angels have never lost their popularity. The Victorians loved painting them, though often in Arthurian rather than religious scenes. It is significant, too, that the most celebrated British statue of modern times also depicts an angel, with its wings outstretched in welcome and protection. The public affection shown for *The Angel of the North* demonstrates that the old tradition remains as strong as ever.

ANGELS
AND RELIGION

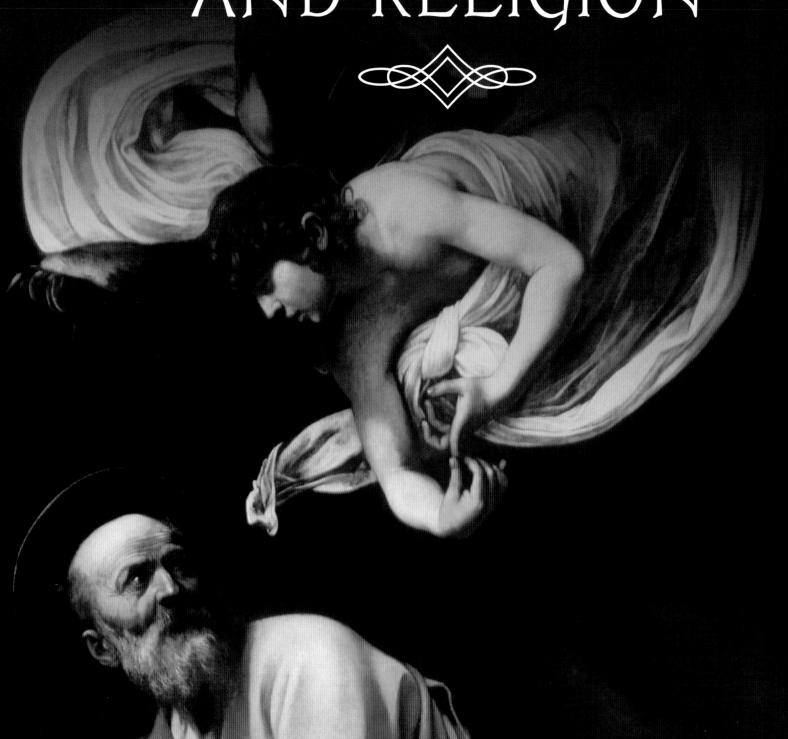

E ver since ancient times, mystical winged beings have been represented in art. Winged humans, creatures and sacred birds, some over 3,000 years old, were depicted by early Middle-Eastern civilizations. These sorts of representations provided prototypes and inspiration for the concept of angels as spiritual messengers in monotheistic religions, for Judaism, Islam and Christianity all include belief in the existence of angels. So it should come as no surprise that this section opens with images of pagan sculpture from ancient Assyria and classical Greece, and an example of Egyptian tomb painting.

Despite the fact that angels are mentioned in the Old Testament, the Jews were prohibited from making religious images for fear these could be used for idolatrous worship, so we have no way of telling what these early Biblical angels looked like. Even after the birth of Christ, this prohibition continued to have an impact on the production of images. As a result, representations of angels are rare until the fifth and sixth centuries, when depictions start to appear in early Christian illuminated manuscripts, mosaics and icons.

In this first section of the book you will see a wide variety of angels in their many roles, as described in sacred texts. There are cherubim and seraphim, archangels and fallen angels. There are angels interceding for God, delivering messages and showing the way to heaven. Some of the best-loved paintings of angels were produced during the Renaissance, which took place during the fifteenth and early sixteenth centuries both in Italy and in Northern Europe. You will also find beautiful examples of Persian manuscript miniatures resplendent with vibrantly coloured winged messengers as angels play a significant role in the teachings of Islam.

Early Prototypes and Old Testament Angels

The earliest prototypes for angels came from the east, and from ancient Mesopotamia in particular. Both the Assyrians and the Babylonians created monumental statues of composite beasts, which included the wings of birds of prey. These served both as guardians and as servants. The Israelites would have become aware of such things in their periods of exile, during the Assyrian and Babylonian Captivity. The winged creatures mentioned in the prophecy of Ezekiel (Ezekiel 1:15–28) certainly appear to stem from this source, as does the folkloric content of parts of the Book of Tobit. Further inspiration came from the sacred birds, which figured in the Egyptian pantheon of gods, and these influences filtered down in turn to the winged statues produced by the Greeks and Romans.

Models of this kind proved useful for later Christian artists, even though they do not appear to be an accurate reflection of the angels mentioned in the Old Testament. In most instances, these seem to be indistinguishable from humans and are presumably wingless. This appears to be the case with the strangers who visit Abraham, while Raphael's disguise in his dealings with Tobias would certainly be more complicated if he was winged.

Winged Bull, eigth century BC
Neo-Assyrian

Some of the earliest ideas about angels came from the eastern neighbours of the Israelites. During the period of the Assyrian Captivity, in the eighth century BC, they would have witnessed at first hand the colossal, winged statues which stood at the entrances of palaces and temples.

This type of being was known as a *shedu* or *lamassu*. It was a guardian spirit, designed to ward off evil influences. Lamassus took the form of a composite creature, combining the body of a bull or lion with the wings of a bird of prey and the head of a man. These features symbolized the spirit's qualities – the strength of a bull, the speed of a bird and the intelligence of a human. The figure wears a horned helmet, to emphasise the divinity of the creature. It also has the unusual feature of five legs. This enabled the beast to present two different viewpoints. From the front, its two visible legs appeared solid and unmoveable while, from the side, the creature appeared to be striding forward, to confront its enemies.

This particular sculpture came from the doorway of a palace at Dur Sharrukin (now Khorsabad). It was built for Sargon II (reigned 721–705 BC), one of the rulers who enslaved the Children of Israel.

Mural on Tomb of Bannantiu, c. 664–525 BC
by an unknown artist

Located in the Bahariyya Oasis in Egypt, the large Tomb of Bannantiu is over 2,000 years old and houses the remains of a wealthy trader or landowner. The interior is decorated in vibrant colours and this detail from the tomb depicts Anubis, the jackal-headed god of the dead, preparing Bannantiu's body on a mummification table.

Anubis holds a vessel over Bannantiu's face, while four canopic jars are positioned on the floor beneath, ready to receive his internal organs.

The goddesses Isis and Nephthys, at either ends of the table, adopt poses of mourning. Depicted hovering above the figures is the 'Ba' of Bannantiu.

The Ba is roughly equivalent to the modern idea of the soul – although this was a far more complex concept in ancient Egypt – and has been compared to a guardian angel. Usually depicted as a sparrowhawk or falcon, chosen for their ability to navigate land, sea and air, the Ba is represented with a human face, sometimes thought to be that of the deceased. The Ba would fly to the land of the living at night, so the dead never lost touch with the world they had left, and always returned to the body it belonged to during the day, bringing air and water.

The Old Testament Trinity, *c.* 1411
by Andrei Rublev (*c.* 1360–1430)

In the West artists normally represented The Trinity with a combination of God the Father, Christ and the Dove representing the Holy Ghost. In the East, however, the icon painters of Russia and Byzantium preferred a rather different version. This stemmed from an episode described in Genesis, when three strangers appeared to Abraham at the grove of Mamre, as 'he sat in the tent door in the heat of the day' (Genesis 18:1). Abraham immediately sensed that these were angels, and he rushed to bring them food and drink. They, in turn, thanked him for his hospitality and informed him that his wife Sarah would bear a child. Even though she was old, this prophecy turned out to be true.

Nowadays this episode is widely interpreted as a foreshadowing of the Last Supper and the Eucharist. This is emphasized by the chalice on the table, while some versions of the theme also show an animal being sacrificed in the foreground. The angels carry wands, to indicate that they have travelled a great distance and, in keeping with icon tradition, their feet rest on raised platforms, to emphasize their divine status. The tree in the background is the Oak of Mamre, an emblem of the Tree of Life.

The Winged Victory of Samothrace, *c.* 190 BC
by an unknown artist

The Greeks and Romans generally portrayed their gods and goddesses without wings. However, there were a few notable exceptions to this rule. The messengers of the gods – figures such as Mercury and Iris – were either winged or had winged apparel. In addition, there was a sizeable group of lesser divinities who were also shown with wings. These figures personified great virtues or important concepts, such as Fame, Fortune and History. Nike or Victory was the most popular of these.

The Greeks portrayed Nike as a winged female figure. In many cases a statue of her was placed in a temple or sanctuary to give thanks to the gods for success in battle. This remarkable Hellenistic statue, discovered on the Aegean island of Samothrace in 1863, is the finest surviving depiction of Victory. It was set on a marble base in the form of a warship, giving the impression that Nike was a figurehead on its prow. The outspread wing and the wind-blown drapery add to this effect. These details also confirm that the statue was designed to commemorate a naval success – perhaps the victory at Side (190 BC), when the islanders of Rhodes overcame a Syrian fleet.

The Sacrifice of Isaac, *c.* 1625–26
by Johann Liss (*c.* 1597–1631)

This dramatic picture records a key episode in the Old Testament. In a
chilling test of faith, God ordered Abraham, one of the great Hebrew
patriarchs, to offer up his son Isaac as a sacrifice to Him. Obediently Abraham
took the youth to the appointed site, built up an altar on which to make the
burnt offering, and then took out his knife. Just as he was about to kill Isaac
an angel of the Lord intervened, saying: 'Lay not thine hand upon the lad,
neither do thou anything unto him; for now I know that thou fearest God,
seeing thou hast not withheld thy son, thine only son from me' (Genesis
22:12). Abraham did as he was told. In place of his son he offered up a ram
that was caught by the horns in a nearby thicket.

Paintings of this subject were frequently commissioned by the Church
authorities who recognized its importance. For the incident is normally
interpreted as a foreshadowing of Christ's sacrifice on the Cross. The ram that
died in Isaac's place was seen as a reference to the Lamb of God (*see* page 79),
while the thorns in the thicket are thought to symbolize the Crown of Thorns.

The Sacrifice of Isaac, 1635
by Rembrandt van Rijn (1606–69)

This is Rembrandt's imaginative reworking of a popular Biblical subject,
described in the Book of Genesis (*see* above). Unlike many of the other
artists who tackled this theme, he laid the emphasis on the appalling
human drama at the centre of the story. The prone figure of Isaac is pushed
right to the front of the picture, underlining the sheer brutality of the
proposed sacrifice. It is also highlighted by the way that the old man's hand
completely covers his son's face, doubtless so that he will not have to look
at it, as he carries out the killing. The falling knife is equally prominent. In
a dark painting, the bright gleam of the blade and its expensive sheath
immediately catch the eye. Unusually, the intervening angel does not look
at Abraham, but gazes instead at the pitiful figure of Isaac. Significantly,
too, there is no sign of the ram, which will be sacrificed in his place.

In the east, icon painters often incorporated a reference to this
incident into their depictions of The Trinity (*see* page 15). While Abraham
is entertaining his holy guests, there is often a scene in the foreground,
showing the sacrifice of an animal.

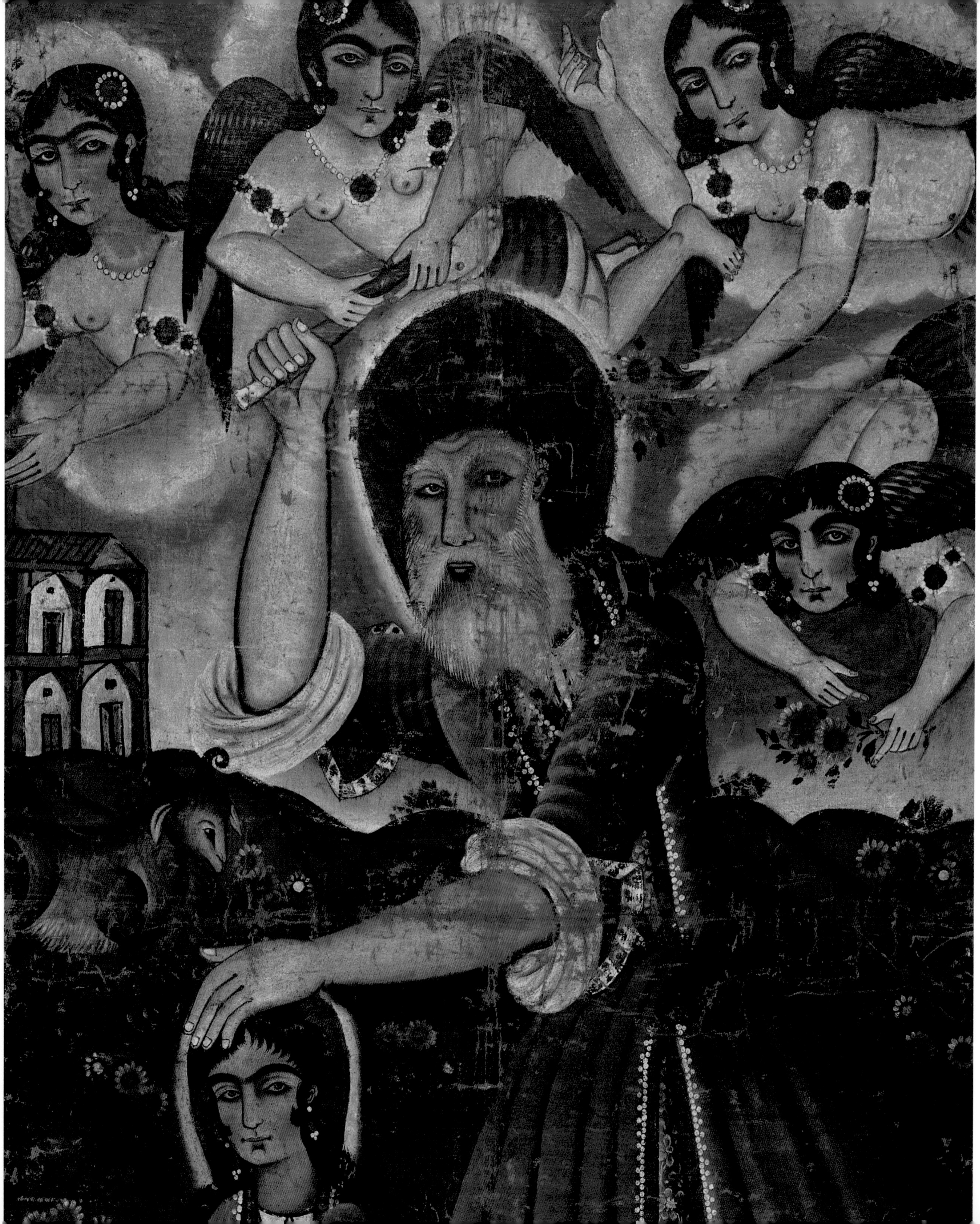

Abraham and Isaac, Persian painting, nineteenth century
by an unknown artist

In this Persian image, Abraham is shown about to offer his son as a sacrifice in response to a request from God, intended to test Abraham's faith. Just as Abraham is about to carry out the sacrifice, an angel prevents him from doing so – although four are depicted here – and provides a ram to sacrifice in place of his son. Christianity and Islam have common origins through Abraham and he appears both in the Bible and the Koran, hence the Middle Eastern origins of this image. Although in the Christian faith the son is referred to as Isaac, in Islam he is often considered to have been Ishmael.

Although many people in the West may consider angels to be solely part of the Christian tradition, angels have an important role in Islam, and belief in the existence of angels is one of the fundamental articles of faith. The Koran teaches that angels are created from light by God for the sole purpose of serving Him and carrying out his commandments. The Arabic word for angel is 'malak', from the word for messenger. Indeed, Muslims believe that it was through the Angel Gabriel (Jibreel) that God revealed his message to the Prophet Muhammad.

Shadrach, Meshach and Abednego in the Fiery Furnace, 1863
by Simeon Solomon (1840–1905)

Solomon's painting illustrates a scene from the Book of Daniel, in the Old Testament. This described how Nebuchadnezzar, the Babylonian ruler, created a golden idol and ordered all his subjects to worship it. Three youths refused, however, and were cast into a fiery furnace. Despite the intense heat all three were unharmed, as an angel protected them. Interestingly, the Biblical passage specified that the angel resembled Christ: 'Lo, I see four men loose, walking in the midst of the fire, and they have no hurt; and the form of the fourth is like the Son of God' (Daniel 3:25).

This subject was portrayed in some of the earliest Christian art. Examples can be found in the Roman Catacombs. However, it became considerably less common after the medieval period. Solomon's version is reminiscent of a *Virgin Misericordia* – a Virgin of Mercy, who shelters a number of smaller figures under her outspread cloak.

Simeon Solomon (1840–1905) belonged to the Pre-Raphaelite circle and was a friend of Sir Edward Burne-Jones (1833–98). His style was strongly influenced by this group, but his Jewish background helped him to provide a new slant on many of the religious subjects that he tackled.

Adam and Eve, fifteenth century
manuscript illumination by unknown artist

Depictions of Adam and Eve historically contain elements of the Biblical narrative told in Genesis. In this manuscript illumination of Adam and Eve, taken from *The Activities of Noble Women and Men*, the couple are depicted twice. At first they are shown to the left, standing next to the Tree of Knowledge, which is covered in an abundance of apples. Satan, disguised as a serpent, coils his body around and up the tree. The serpent's face has a human image. Eve holds one apple in her hand. It is clear that she has eaten part of the fruit because she holds a tree branch in front of her lower body, a symbol of carnal knowledge.

On the right-hand side of the manuscript Adam and Eve are at the exit of the Garden of Eden. The bible states that the 'Lord God sent him [Adam] forth from the Garden of Eden… at the east of the garden of Eden he placed a cherubim, and a flaming sword, which turned every way to guard the tree of life.' The artist places the winged angel above Adam and Eve. His large sword is held in a strike position, as a warning to the couple.

The Expulsion from Paradise, c. 1425–28
by Masaccio (1401–28)

In his all too brief career, Masaccio (1401–28) became a founding father of the Renaissance and this groundbreaking fresco, produced for Brancacci Chapel, in the church of Santa Maria del Carmine in Florence, was one of his key achievements. It illustrates the passage from Genesis (3:23–24), when God expelled Adam and Eve from the Garden of Eden, leaving cherubims to guard the entrance.

Masaccio's treatment of the subject has a psychological depth that was lacking in earlier versions. The couple are not intimidated by the angel – they barely seem aware of it. Instead, they cover their faces and their bodies, racked with guilt and shame at their terrible sin. The nakedness of the figures would have come as a shock to Masaccio's contemporaries. The Biblical text specifies that the Lord made 'coats of skins and clothed them' (Genesis 3:21), but this approach accentuated their humiliation (*see* pages 32–33). Masaccio's mastery of the new technique of perspective gave the scene an added sense of reality. The anatomical accuracy of the figures and the shadows that they cast are far more convincing than anything that had gone before.

ADAM AND EVE, c. 1550
ascribed to Ja'far al-Sadiq, from a copy of the Falnama, or Book of Omens

This beatiful illumination comes from a manuscript from the royal court of Qazvin, Persia (Iran), capital at the time of the Safavid empire, a Shi'a dynasty that ruled the Persian empire from 1501 to 1722. This was a period of great cultural activity during which the painting of miniatures thrived and where the prohibition of the depiction of human forms had less force than in other Islamic countries.

Muslims believe that Adam is the father of human-kind and the first prophet. Here he is depicted astride a huge dragon-like serpent, while Eve follows him on a peacock, the gatekeeper of Paradise. Iblis, the Islamic equivalent of Satan, has flattered the peacock into allowing the serpent into Paradise, while Iblis hides between its fangs. Once inside Paradise, he will tempt Eve into eating the forbidden fruit of the Tree of Knowledge.

The heads of Adam and Eve are surrounded by sacred fire – the equivalent of a halo – and they ride across a stylized grassy area that looks like a Persian carpet, with a band of angels on either side. As we saw in *Abraham and Isaac* on page 18, angels play an important part in the Islamic faith. In this work, produced around 300 years earlier, they are depicted with brightly coloured wings, like those of tropical birds, and are dressed in the lavish courtly clothing of the day.

The Expulsion of Adam and Eve, date unknown
by Thomas Stothard (1755–1834)

Stothard's picture is a fairly literal depiction of the passage in the Book of Genesis when Adam and Eve were cast out of paradise: 'So he drove out the man; and he placed at the east of the garden of Eden Cherubims, and a flaming sword which turned every way, to keep the way of the tree of life' (Genesis 3:24). This term for 'angel' derives from the Hebrew word *k'rubim*. This originally referred to a lower order of Babylonian deities who mediated between humanity and the higher gods. In ancient sculpture they were represented by winged lions or bulls with human heads.

Thomas Stothard was a versatile painter and designer, but it was as a book illustrator that he really made his name. As he did not engrave his own plates, he managed to produce an enormous output during the course of his lengthy career. He excelled at depicting narrative scenes, conveying them with simplicity and a genteel refinement that won him many admirers, not to mention imitators. Most of his paintings were on a small scale, although he also executed imposing decorative schemes at Burghley House, near Peterborough, and at the Advocates' Library, Edinburgh.

Expulsion from Paradise, nineteenth century
by Alexandre Cabanel (1823–89)

Cabanel's depiction of the expulsion of Adam and Eve is set a little earlier than the work on pages 26–27. God has arrived in the Garden of Eden, ready to deliver his judgment on the sinful couple. He is accompanied by the cherubim, who will guard the entrance to Paradise, to prevent Adam and Eve from returning. In addition to their function as divine protectors, cherubims were sometimes shown bearing God on their wings. Several references to this can be found in the Bible, among them a passage in the Book of Samuel: 'And He rode upon a cherub, and did fly: and He was seen upon the wings of the wind' (2 Samuel 22:11).

Cabanel was a successful Salon artist, who built his reputation on his skill at portraying the human figure. It is no surprise, therefore, that he chose the nude studies of Adam and Eve as the main focus of this painting. Eve, in particular, appears under the spotlight. Cabanel portrayed her in the same manner as his mythological characters so that she resembles a startled nymph or goddess. In spite of his immense popularity, the artist's fame faded swiftly following his death.

O Adam, One Almighty Is, From Whom All Things Proceed, 1866
by Gustave Doré (1832–83)

This image is one plate from a nineteenth-century edition of *Paradise Lost* by the English poet John Milton (1608–74). The epic poem dramatizes the Fall of Man. Milton's first edition of 1667 printed the epic in ten books. This plate illustrates the Archangel Raphael visiting Adam and Eve in Adam's bower in the Garden of Eden in Paradise. Satan had tempted Eve in a dream and she was troubled by it. Archangel Raphael is a messenger between Heaven and Earth. God has sent Raphael to bring the word of God to Man. He warns Adam and Eve of the dangers of Satan. The couple are depicted listening to him, his arm raised to Heaven to explain how Satan was expelled after his revolt against God. He warns that although they are made perfect they are not immutable. They should be on their guard against Satan's temptations.

The meeting between Adam, Eve and Archangel Raphael is of Milton's making. It does not appear in the Bible. The scene illustrates his prose: 'To whom the winged Hierarch replied, "O Adam, one Almighty is, from whom All things proceed" (Book 5, 468–70, plate 22).' Gustave Doré was a successful French graphic artist, painter and sculptor.

Adam and Eve, 1896
William Morris (1834–96)

William Morris (1834–96) revitalized English design, emphasizing the importance of genuine craftsmanship and its superiority over mass-production. He applied this philosophy to many different fields, from furniture and wallpapers to textiles and ceramics. His last great project was the creation of a private press, to reinvigorate the process of book production. Founded in 1890, the Kelmscott Press was the realization of Morris's dream. *Adam and Eve* comes from his edition of *Chaucer*, which W.B. Yeats described as 'the most beautiful of all printed books'.

Most of the illustrations were a collaboration between Morris and Edward Burne-Jones (1833–98), with the latter providing the images while Morris concentrated on the borders. The depiction of Eden is deliberately archaic, mimicking the naive illustrations that can be found in early manuscripts (*see* page 20). The Garden is conceived as a tiny, walled enclosure, while the figures are gigantic, symbolizing their importance. Burne-Jones developed a very individual style of angel, which was graceful and elongated, with glorious plumage. This proved highly influential in the nineteenth century, partly because of his paintings, but also because, in partnership with Morris, he produced scores of designs for stained-glass windows.

Tobias and the Angel, c. 1470–80
by the Workshop of Andrea del Verrocchio (c. 1435–88)

The tale of Tobias and the Angel is recounted in one of the texts in the Apocrypha, the Book of Tobit. Young Tobias is sent on a perilous journey by his blind father (Tobit) to recover a debt on his behalf. He is accompanied by the archangel Raphael, who is disguised in human form, calling himself Azarias. On the way he catches a miraculous fish, which helps to cure his father's blindness (*see* Savoldo page 30). In this scene the angel is carrying the magic ingredients in a golden box, while the boy holds the fish itself and a document relating to the debt. Because of his links with this famous story Raphael became one of the prototypes for the concept of the guardian angel.

Paintings of Tobias and the Angel were especially popular in Florence where the Confraternity of Saint Raphael was a flourishing organization. Founded by a goldsmith in 1409 it was a charitable institution that sponsored religious education for the young.

Although he was a fine sculptor in his own right, Andrea del Verrocchio (c. 1435–88) is chiefly famous for having trained Leonardo da Vinci (1452–1519). Inevitably historians have looked for signs of the latter's involvement in this picture and there have been suggestions that he painted the dog.

Tobias and the Angel, 1542
by Giovanni Girolamo Savoldo (fl. 1506–48)

This is the central episode in the story of Tobias and the Angel. While he was travelling under the protection of the archangel Raphael, Tobias was attacked and almost eaten by a 'great fish'. He managed to kill it, however, and was then instructed by the angel to remove its liver, heart, and gall. When prepared in a special way these ingredients helped to cure his father's blindness.

The 'great fish' in question was probably a crocodile. It had the necessary aggression and, more importantly, its innards were traditionally used in ancient charms. In western art though, the creature was always depicted as a normal fish. The portrayal of the angel also required some artistic licence. In the original text Raphael kept his identity a secret and the lad had no idea that his travelling companion was an angel. Despite this, western artists normally included his wings, to make the identification of the subject easier.

Savoldo was an Italian artist, probably from Brescia, though he spent most of his career in Venice. He is mainly remembered for his night scenes, which have an unusual, poetic quality, and for his immense skill at depicting drapery, which is clearly evident from Raphael's elaborate costume.

The Angel Raphael leaving Tobit and his Family, 1637
by Rembrandt van Rijn (1606–69)

Rembrandt produced several paintings and etchings on subjects drawn from the Book of Tobit but, unlike most artists (*see* pages 29–30), he preferred to concentrate on Tobit himself rather than his young son. This scene occurs after Tobias and his friend have returned from their journey bringing a cure for the old man's blindness. Naturally Tobit and his family are overcome with a mixture of joy and amazement. In the midst of their celebrations, however, they receive an even bigger surprise when Tobias's companion reveals himself as the archangel Raphael.

The Book of Tobit was probably written in the second century BC, although it is set in an even earlier period (eighth century BC). It reflects a time when the Israelites were living in exile from their homeland. As a

result the text betrays strong influences of folk traditions from eastern lands such as Assyria and Babylonia. This produced one unexpected benefit for western artists – it gave them an opportunity to try their hand at painting dogs. The ancient Jews regarded dogs as unclean so the animal is rarely mentioned in the Scriptures. It was included in the story of Tobias, however, and became an ever present feature in paintings of this subject.

Gabriel and the Annunciation

First and foremost, angels were messengers, the most important line of communication between God and humanity. In the New Testament, the most important herald is the archangel Gabriel. He was revered by Christians, Jews and Muslims. In artistic terms, he is chiefly associated with the Annunciation, although he has also been linked with several of the unnamed angels in the Scriptures. The most prominent of these are the angelic messenger, who announced the birth of the Christ to the shepherds, and the angel who met with the three Maries at Christ's sepulchre, following His resurrection. In the Old Testament, he has been associated with the destruction of Sodom and the burial of Moses.

The Annunciation is one of the most widely represented themes in Christian art. Its importance was recognized by the Church at a very early stage and it was granted its feast day (March 25) at around the time of the Council of Ephesus (*c.* 431). In Britain, this is also known as Lady Day. Pictures of this episode usually signify more than Gabriel's announcement. In most cases, they also portray the Incarnation itself. This occurs when the rays of light emanating from the Dove – the Holy Spirit – reach the Virgin.

The Annunciation, *c.* 1430–32
by Fra Angelico (*c.* 1395–1455)

Fra Angelico produced many paintings of The Annunciation over the course of his career, reworking the same formula with slight variations. This particular version was created for the monastery of San Domenico at Fiesole, with which he had close links; he joined the Dominican order there and was later appointed as its prior (1450). The painting is now in the Prado, in Madrid.

Fra Angelico's religious background led him to emphasize the doctrinal significance of his subject. So, while many artists portrayed The Annunciation in a fairly naturalistic manner, depicting Mary's surprise at the sudden appearance of an angel, his Virgin adopts a pious pose, bowing slightly and crossing herself. Fra Angelico also took the unusual step of including Adam and Eve's expulsion from Paradise as part of the same scene. In his role as a preacher he was stressing that Christ's coming was a direct result of the Fall, and that without His sacrifice the souls of Adam and Eve and their descendants would have dwelt forever in limbo. Their inclusion also gives a new dimension to the garden setting. In many Annunciations this represented the *hortus conclusus* – the walled garden – which was a traditional symbol of the Virgin's chastity. Here, however, it doubles as the Garden of Eden.

The Angel of the Annunciation, 1437
by Fra Angelico (c. 1395–1455)

Many altarpieces illustrated more than one episode from the Scriptures, creating a narrative for the spectator. The central panel provided the main focus of the religious message, and this was amplified in secondary themes, depicted in side-panels or a *predella* (literally 'a platform', a small painting underneath the principal scene). Thus in Fra Angelico's Prado *Annunciation* (*see* pages 32–33), the predella features tiny depictions of other key episodes in Mary's life: *The Birth and Marriage of the Virgin*, *The Visitation*, *The Presentation in the Temple*, and *The Death of the Virgin*.

In this instance the Annunciation is one of the subsidiary themes. It forms part of Fra Angelico's altarpiece for the chapel of San Niccolo dei Guidalotti, in the church of San Domenico in Perugia. Here the main panel is a portrait of the *Virgin and Child. The Annunciation* is shown in two separate roundels, on either side of the central panel. It would be difficult to reduce most Biblical themes to such a stripped-down format, but the kneeling pose and the raised hand instantly suggest the Annunciation. To confirm the identification the angel carries a palm frond, a conventional symbol of Christ's victory over death. In his Prado *Annunciation*, Fra Angelico included a palm tree in the garden.

The Annunciation, 1489–90
by Sandro Botticelli (c. 1445–1510)

Botticelli painted several versions of *The Annunciation*, but this is probably the best known. It was produced for the chapel of Benedetto Guardi, in the church of Santa Maria Maddelena de' Pazzi in Florence. The most striking aspect of the picture is the dramatic, defensive pose of the Virgin, as she suddenly notices the arrival of the angel. This emotionalism is in marked contrast to Botticelli's other Annunciations, where she receives the news in a calm, dignified manner, and this has led to suggestions that the artist was already falling under the spell of the fiery preacher, Savonarola (1452–98).

In common with many of Botticelli's other angels, Gabriel is portrayed as a graceful youth. He carries a lily, a conventional symbol of Mary's purity. His most curious feature is his halo; this is depicted as a flat disc, similar to the Virgin's, but as it is seen from the side, it is barely apparent.

The view outside the window shows a walled garden, another emblem of Mary's chastity, while the tree has been interpreted as a reference to the Tree of Jesse, which signified Christ's descent from the house of David. The cityscape in the distance was influenced by Northern European versions of this subject.

The Annunciation, 1480–85
by Lorenzo di Credi (c. 1458–1537)

The setting of the Annunciation varied considerably in Renaissance art. The Gospels specify that Gabriel 'came in unto' Mary, which suggests that the sacred event took place indoors. Many painters, however, preferred to set it in the open air, either in a portico or loggia. Either way, there was usually a view out onto a garden. One reason for this was to emphasize that the Annunciation took place in the spring, to tie in with the nativity in winter.

Because of her key role in the redemption of humanity, Mary was sometimes described as 'the Second Eve'. This link is highlighted by the three scenes beneath *The Annunciation*. On the left, there is a depiction of *The Creation of Eve*, showing her emerging from Adam's side, while he sleeps. *The Temptation* is in the centre and, to its right, *The Expulsion from the Garden of Eden*. The ornamental pillars, which separate the scenes, echo the decoration of the Virgin's chamber. However, the jarring perspective of the main scene, where the floor appears to rise, and the lower tier, where the events are seen head-on, gives the impression that *The Annunciation* is taking place at the edge of a stage.

The Annunciation, 1546
by Pomponio Amalteo (1505–88)

This painting belongs to an altarpiece of *The Annunciation*, which can now be found in the Chapel of St Donato, in the Cathedral of Cividale del Friuli, although it was originally produced for a nearby monastery.

Amalteo's composition is an uncomfortable mix of tradition and innovation. After the Council of Trent (1545), which effectively launched the Counter Reformation, it became increasingly common to include a swarm of cherubs in subjects of this kind. Here, they lift and transport God the Father in his heavenly domain. Earlier artists had also emphasized that Gabriel's message came from God, but usually in a more subtle manner. In Fra Angelico's *Annunciation*, for example, (*see* pages 32–33), God's head is included as a roundel in the architecture.

The setting shown here is a rather grandiose, classical version of the Temple of Jerusalem. According to an old tradition, which stemmed from the apocryphal gospels and was popularized in *The Golden Legend* (a medieval anthology of religious texts), Mary grew up and was educated there. As a young woman, one of her chief duties was to look after the vestments worn by the priests. Amalteo makes reference to this by including a variety of sewing materials in a basket by the Virgin's feet.

The Annunciation (detail), c. 1583–95
by Annibale Carracci (1560–1609)

The archangel Gabriel is frequently portrayed in western art, although he is only mentioned by name four times in the Bible. In the Old Testament, he appeared in the Book of Daniel, while in the Gospels he acted as a herald, foretelling the births of John the Baptist and Christ. Traditionally though, he is also identified with many of the unnamed angels in the Scriptures. Among other things, it has been suggested that he was the angelic spirit who reassured Joseph after Mary's conception, who summoned the shepherds to the scene of Christ's nativity, and who sounded the horn on Judgment Day.

Gabriel is also revered by Jews and Muslims. In Hebrew his name means 'God is my strength' and he was sometimes portrayed as the instrument of divine punishment. The destruction of Sodom, for example, was traditionally ascribed to him. At the same time, he was also identified as the angel who instructed Noah to bring the animals into the Ark, and as one of the angels who helped to bury Moses.

In Islamic tradition Gabriel's name was Jibreel. His chief significance was as the angel who revealed the Koran to the prophet Muhammad. He also stood at the north-eastern corner of the Ka'aba, Islam's most sacred shrine.

The Annunciation, 1604
by El Greco (c. 1541–1614)

During the Counter Reformation, when the Catholic establishment tried to stem the tide of Protestantism, there was a profound change in the character of religious painting. There was a new emphasis on spirituality and emotional

intensity, which overrode the old tendency to dwell on the precise details of the Gospel accounts, or to repeat traditional symbols and compositions. No artist adapted to these changes more successfully than El Greco. His gaunt, elongated figures, his eerie colours, and his shimmering, flame-like forms combined to evoke a sense of mystic rapture in his paintings.

El Greco produced numerous versions of *The Annunciation*, often with the heavenly host appearing in the sky. This is one of his more restrained examples. Even so, the artist has swept away the earthly setting of the event and replaced it with a visionary aura. Gabriel arrives on a cloud, while the dove representing the Holy Ghost descends in a searing flash of light. The Virgin is accompanied by just two traditional elements – the lily and the book. According to St Bernard, the latter was open at a prophetic passage in the Old Testament, which read: 'Behold, a virgin shall conceive, and bear a son' (Isaiah 7:14).

The Annunciation, 1657
by Nicolas Poussin (1594–1665)

Poussin was the supreme exponent of the classical style, renowned for producing paintings that were both morally uplifting and immaculately constructed. There can be no finer example of these qualities than this austere depiction of *The Annunciation*. The mood is serious to the point of being sombre, while the figures resemble statues, with not a movement or a gesture out of place.

In an era when images of the Annunciation often contained a chorus of smaller angels, Poussin's version is reduced to its barest essentials. Gabriel's white garb, his pointing hand, and the open book are all conventional features, though the Virgin's yellow robe is an unexplained departure from tradition. Her eyes are closed, rapt in a vision, and her submission to the sacred experience is every bit as wholehearted as Bernini's *Saint Teresa* (*see* pages 114–15). The most unusual feature, perhaps, is the dove. Most painters depicted this in a naturalistic way, flying down from heaven to complete the incarnation of Christ. Here though, the bird hovers above Mary, its wings outstretched to form the sign of the cross. Its aura creates a halo over the Virgin's head.

It has been suggested that this painting was commissioned for the tomb of Cassiano dal Pozzo (1588–1657), Poussin's chief patron. If so, this might help to account for the picture's solemn mood.

POVSSIN·FACIEBAT·

The Annunciation, 1888
by William Adolphe Bouguereau (1825–1905)

The Annunciation is principally related in the Gospel of Saint Luke, although artists often borrowed further details from the Apocrypha or the *Golden Legend*, a medieval anthology of Christian material. The Feast of the Annunciation, also known as Lady Day, is celebrated on 25 March.

Usually Mary and Gabriel are shown facing each other, with the virgin often displaying some surprise at the sudden appearance of the angel. This natural human reaction is notably absent from Bouguereau's austere version of the subject. The figures face the spectator, but their gaze is downcast. Both are absorbed in the spiritual significance of the event and pay no heed to their material surroundings. The traditional symbols of the Annunciation are lined up in the foreground, instead of being integrated into the scene. The spinning wheel and the basket of wool allude to the virgin's upbringing in the Temple of Jerusalem, where tradition has it that she was given the task of making vestments for the priests. The flowering shrub emphasizes that the Annunciation took place in the springtime.

The Annunciation, 1901
by F. Pickford Marriott (1860–1941)

This remarkable artwork is a triumph of style over content. The holy scene is imaginatively recast as a harmonious, symmetrical design. Gabriel, on the right, delivers his message, pointing upwards to indicate that it comes from God. He wears a crown, signifying that he is chief of the angelic host. Facing him Mary is surrounded by a swirl of infant angels' heads, emphasizing the theme of maternity. Unusually, the focus of the picture is the lily. This symbolizes the virgin's purity and is also Gabriel's personal attribute. It is encircled by a shaft of golden light, emanating from the holy spirit. Traditionally this was directed at the virgin's head, but here it reaches her as she touches the flower.

Marriott was born in Stoke-on-Trent and at the age of 14 began work as a pottery painter. He worked in a wide variety of media including wood-carving, repoussé work and enamelling, although his most memorable works are probably his gesso panels. Marriott was a member of both the Art Workers' Guild and the Arts and Crafts Society, but also exhibited at the Royal Academy and the Salon. In later life he became a teacher.

THE ANNVNCIATION

The Annunciation, 1914
by John William Waterhouse (1849–1917)

The Pre-Raphaelites and their successors tried to instil a greater sense of realism into their religious pictures. In doing so they were following the advice of the critic, John Ruskin (1819–1900), who urged painters to portray the virgin as 'a simple Jewish girl', rather than 'a graceful princess crowned with gems'.

Waterhouse's remarkable version of the subject certainly breathed new life into the theme, avoiding many of the old clichés. He portrays the virgin as a young woman rather than a sacred icon. Her pose is very natural, reflecting her obvious surprise at seeing an angel appear out of nowhere. The setting is presented in an equally novel fashion, even though it manages to include several of the customary symbols. Traditionally the virgin is kneeling at a prie-dieu when Gabriel arrives. On it there is a text from the Old Testament prophesying the coming of the Saviour. According to Saint Bernard this came from Isaiah: 'Behold a virgin shall conceive, and bear a son' (Isaiah 7:14). Often, as here, there is a distaff (a stick for spinning thread) by the virgin's side. This alludes to the legend that Mary was raised at the Temple in Jerusalem, where she made vestments for the priests.

ECCE ANCILLA DOMINI, DATE UNKNOWN
BY EDWARD A. FELLOWES-PRYNNE (1854–1921)

This sumptuously coloured version of the Annunciation
follows a traditional format, employing a symbolic formula that
had been in use since the Middle Ages. The archangel
Gabriel arrives on a cloud, bringing Mary the news
that she has been chosen by God to be the mother of Christ.
His words are also shown on a strip of material, which hangs from
his costume, 'Ave gratis plena Dominus tecum' ('Greetings most
favoured one! The Lord is with you', Luke 1:28). The virgin,
meanwhile, holds her hand to her breast and utters the words
'Ecce ancilla domini' ('Here I am. I am the Lord's servant', Luke 1:38)
thereby accepting her destiny. At the top of the picture a ray of light
beams down from the dove, which symbolizes the Holy Spirit. The light
itself represents the Incarnation of Christ. When the beam touches
her head, this is the moment of conception. Mary's purity is
symbolized both by the lily and by the fence behind her.
This indicates that she is standing in a *hortus conclusus*
('enclosed garden'), a traditional symbol of virginity.
On the right-hand side, the apple on the wall refers to
the temptation of Eve. Mary was described by
theologians as the second Eve, because of her part
in bringing about the redemption of humanity.

Nativity, Madonna and Child

Angels feature prominently in the events surrounding Christ's birth. The gospels relate how Gabriel announced this to the shepherds, as they guarded their flocks, and how his words were accompanied by the sudden appearance of the heavenly host. Descriptions of the Nativity itself are less detailed, but artists frequently embellished the scene, either with angelic rejoicing or with angels who knelt alongside Mary to worship the newborn Saviour. Painters also added angels to pictures of The Flight into Egypt, when the holy family fled from Herod's soldiers. They were often shown protecting them as they began their journey, or bringing them food when they stopped to rest on the way.

Angels also made a frequent appearance in paintings of the Virgin and Child. The basic format of this subject originated in Byzantium, but became far more elaborate in the West, where it was often commissioned by private patrons as a devotional picture. Since there was no specific Biblical text to follow artists had considerable scope for invention. If angels were included they could be any size or any age. The more conventional examples were simple attendants or musicians, but artists often preferred to show their angelic infants acting like real children, to make the scene more convincing.

Mystic Nativity, 1500
by Sandro Botticelli (c. 1445–1510)

This enigmatic version of the *Nativity* is one of Botticelli's strangest pictures. It depicts the joyous celebrations which occurred, both in heaven and on earth, following the birth of Jesus. However, it also refers to prophecies in the Book of Revelation, which relate to the second coming of Christ.

The setting for this miraculous event is a bizarre structure, which is part cave and part manger. The notion that the Nativity took place in a cave derives from the apocryphal Book of James. It was rarely depicted in the West, although it was a conventional feature of icons produced in the East. The landscape in front of this structure is apocalyptic, with great fissures appearing in the earth. Some demons can be seen scampering away into these openings. One of them peers out in alarm at the embracing figures in the foreground, aware perhaps that this reconciliation between heaven and humanity signals the end of Satan's influence.

At the top of the picture, Botticelli added a Greek inscription, which has tended to confuse rather than clarify the issue. Part of it reads: 'I Alessandro, in the half-time after the time, painted, according to the eleventh chapter of Saint John, in the second woe of the Apocalypse, during the release of the devil...'

The Adoration of the Shepherds, sixteenth century
by Marcello Venusti (1512/15–79)

Artists often added celestial groups of angels to religious paintings simply for effect, but in scenes of the Nativity there is some basis in the Scriptures for this feature. According to St Luke's gospel, the angel of the Lord – unnamed in the Biblical account, but traditionally identified as Gabriel – appeared to the shepherds, while they were tending their flocks. He announced the birth of Christ to them, after which the scene changed dramatically. 'And suddenly there was with the angel a multitude of the heavenly host praising God, and saying, Glory to God in the highest, and on earth peace, good will toward men' (Luke 2:13–14). Venusti has illustrated this passage in a highly literal fashion. He has even shown the angels holding a long scroll, which carries a Latin translation of their greeting. Most of the shepherds seem oblivious to the angels, but the one on the far left gazes up at them.

In most versions of this subject, the shepherds bring a number of gifts for the newborn Child. These usually include a lamb, here displayed prominently in the foreground. Apart from being a natural gift for a shepherd, this was also a reminder of Christ's future sacrifice as the Lamb of God.

The Nativity (detail of The Nativity with Saints Alexander of Brescia, Jerome, Gaudioso and Filippo Benizzi), c. 1524
by Girolamo Romanino (1484–1562)

The Nativity with Saints Alexander of Brescia, Jerome, Gaudioso and Filippo Benizzi was painted as the central panel of the high altarpiece for the Church of Santo Alessandro in Brescia, Italy. The lateral panels (not shown) depict the four Saints. The main panel (shown here), depicts the Nativity scene, set in a stone arched stable. The infant Jesus lies in a manger, looked upon by Joseph and Mary. They kneel at his crib with an ox and donkey close to the baby in a protective group. Above the parents and baby a group of cherubic winged angels, mystic personifications of God, hover in a cloud from heaven, to welcome and protect Jesus, and to confirm that he is the Son of God. Romanino depicts the rejoicing angels as naked infants, to mirror the innocence of the newborn. Their feathery wings are vividly defined. In the biblical narration a group of angels appear to shepherds caring for the flocks of sheep in fields close to the stables, to tell them that on this day a Saviour, who is Christ the Lord, is born. The fields, shepherd and sheep can be seen in the distance through the arch. The richly coloured work is typical of Venetian painting.

Rucellai Madonna, 1285
by Duccio di Buoninsegna (*c.* 1255–1319)

This is one of the earliest known works by the Sienese painter, Duccio. It takes its name from the Rucellai family, who commissioned the picture for their chapel in Santa Maria Novella, in Florence. At this stage, Italian painting was still heavily influenced by Byzantine art, and many altarpieces were highly reminiscent of icons. This is most noticeable from the way that artists concentrated on the spiritual and symbolic essence of their subjects, and made few efforts to portray them in a realistic fashion.

The painting shows the Madonna enthroned in heaven. She is attended by six angels, as well as a number of saints, whose heads are depicted in tiny roundels on the frame. The gold background, which was typical for this period, adds to the richness of the scene, but also creates a number of ambiguities. It is unclear, for example, whether the angels are simply kneeling in adoration, whether they are supporting the throne, or indeed whether they are raising it up. The lower pair of angels are firmly planted on the platform of the throne, but the remainder seem to float in space – even though this is contradicted by their kneeling pose.

Madonna and Child with Angels, *c.* 1455
by Fra Filippo Lippi (*c.* 1406–69)

Paintings of the Madonna and Child are extremely common, but they can convey very different moods and shades of meaning. Here the Virgin is shown in a contemplative pose, with her hands clasped in prayer. Her sad expression hints that she may already know her Son's fate, a suggestion that is reinforced by the way that Christ reaches across, as if to comfort her. Angels are relatively unusual in this type of subject, but this pair fulfil a number of functions. At a purely practical level, they solve the problem of Mary's praying hands, which obviously cannot hold the Child. More importantly, they also involve the spectator in the scene. The Virgin and Child are absorbed in their own spiritual world, but the angel in the foreground gazes directly at the viewer. His cheerful expression confirms that this scene is a cause for celebration.

Fra Filippo Lippi was raised as an orphan in a friary and later joined the order. He had no vocation for the Church, however, and caused a scandal when he had an affair with a nun, Lucrezia Buti. Both were subsequently released from their vows. Lucrezia is thought to be the model for the Virgin in this picture.

Madonna and Child with Two Angels, c. 1480
by Hans Memling (1430–94)

In this beautiful Northern Renaissance painting, Mary is depicted flanked by two angels holding musical instruments. The left-hand angel holds a viol, a forerunner of the modern violin, while the right-hand angel plays the harp, a symbol of divine music. Both of these instruments are common attributes of angels, who in turn are associated with the production of heavenly music, in the form of singing and instrumental music, to honour God.

The left-hand angel holds out an apple for the infant Christ, who stretches out willingly to take it. An apple is traditionally the emblem of original sin, although the actual type of fruit is not specified in the Bible. However, here the meaning is that Christ, even as a baby, is accepting his future role as mankind's redeemer and saviour, taking on the burden of original sin. Unusually, this angel is dressed as a priest, wearing a dalmatic or deacon's vestment. We are intended to compare this act to a solemn mass, with an angel instead of a priest acting as the intermediary between God and man. The angel on the right wears the more usual alb, or white vestment. Tiny cherubs support the swags that form a symbolic canopy over the head of the Madonna.

Madonna and Child with Cherubs, c. 1485
by Andrea Mantegna (1431–1506)

The infant Christ stands on the Madonna's lap, set against a background of a clouded sky populated with singing cherubs. Clouds can be seen as a symbol of mystery – they conceal heaven and thus the unseen God. Cherubs, or cherubim, are often depicted as winged children, signifying innocence and purity. They represent divine wisdom, they know God and worship him and are described in the Bible as God's throne bearers.

The presence of these cherubim in the same image as the infant Christ invites us to draw comparisions between the two – he is both human and divine, a child who is also angelic and pure, who is innocent yet foresees his fate and knows God. Cherubim are often coloured red or blue, although here most of the faces and wings are naturally coloured. Two pairs of wings, however, are red, symbolizing fire and the burning love of cherubim.

Seraphim, often depicted with cherubim, tend to be depicted in blue to symbolize their association with heaven, although these colours may be reversed, and we often see blue cherubim and red seraphim in paintings.

Madonna of the Pomegranate, c. 1487
by Sandro Botticelli (c. 1445–1510)

The mood of this type of subject can vary considerably. Some are joyous, some are maternal, and some, like this one, are sombre. Botticelli offered a significant clue to this by placing a pomegranate in the Child's hand. This fruit was a traditional symbol of the Resurrection – an idea which stemmed ultimately from its association with the legend of Persephone and Demeter. As a result, the participants in this scene are all fully aware of Christ's future sacrifice, and this accounts for their sober, reflective expressions.

Many images of the Virgin and Child have younger angels, who might almost serve as playmates for the infant Christ, but it is entirely appropriate to feature more mature ones here. The young men have very individual faces, which may well be portraits of courtiers or relations of one of Botticelli's princely patrons. They also have wings, although these scarcely seem adequate from an aerodynamic point of view. The angel on the left is wearing crossed sashes, which bear the words 'Ave Grazia Plena'. This is a line from the *Hail Mary*, referring back to the Annunciation (*see page 42*). The prominent lilies are a conventional symbol of the Virgin, but are also the emblem of Florence, which has fuelled speculation that the painting may have been produced for a public building in the city.

Angels and the Holy Child, 1893
by Marianne Stokes (1855–1927)

Stokes once commented that the defining influences on her art came from an illustrated edition of Grimm's Fairy Tales given to her as a child, and her lifelong study of Catholic ritual. Her artistic education was equally diverse. Born in Austria, she trained in Munich and Paris, where she developed a naturalistic, academic style. She then painted in Brittany, where she met her husband, the British artist Adrian Stokes (1854–1935), and subsequently in the artistic colonies of Skagen and St Ives. A visit to Italy in 1891 inspired her to take up religious painting. For this she adopted a deliberately archaic style, mimicking the early Italians. She also experimented with early techniques, joining the newly formed Society of Painters in Tempera.

Many of these different influences can be detected in this unusual, pared-down version of the Nativity. There are no kings or shepherds and no ox or ass in this manger. The mood is one of contemplation rather than celebration, perhaps focusing on Christ's eventual sacrifice. The use of haloes and the medieval instruments recall early Italian altarpieces; the angelic children have a Pre-Raphaelite flavour; while the virgin's dreamy expression owes a debt to the contemporary Symbolist style.

The Coronation and Assumption of the Virgin

As the cult of the Virgin gathered pace artists devised new ways of glorifying her. Most of these themes had very little basis in the Bible but were drawn from a number of apocryphal texts, many of which were collected in the *Golden Legend* (*see* page 39). The sequence begins with The Death of the Virgin. This was sometimes foretold by an angel in a scene resembling a reprise of The Annunciation. Angels might also be shown carrying the apostles on a cloud so that they could be at the Virgin's side in her final hours. Her death occurs in the middle of the night, when Christ appears 'with sweet melody and song, with the orders of angels'.

The Assumption of the Virgin takes place three days after her death, when her resurrected form is lifted up from the tomb by a company of angels. The presence of the angels is essential, to distinguish the Assumption ('taking up') of Mary from the unaided Ascension of Christ. The angels sometimes play music or form a mandorla (an almond-shaped frame) around her. Once in heaven the Virgin is crowned by Christ or God the Father, confirming her new role as the Queen of Heaven.

Coronation of the Virgin with Saints, 1492
by Domenico Ghirlandaio (1449–94), and Sandro Botticelli (1445–1510)

The Coronation of the Virgin is not narrated in the Bible. Its depiction in art is loosely based on Psalm 44:11-12, and a text attributed to Bishop Melito of Sardis. The Coronation is part of the iconography of the Virgin that includes the Death of the Virgin, the Burial and the Assumption to heaven, and is where Mary, Mother of Jesus, is crowned Queen of Heaven. In this representation by Domenico Ghirlandaio and Sandro Botticelli the Holy Father and t he Virgin appear on a cloud, supported by three winged angels, fully dressed in red, green and white. Below, on Earth, Saints look up to watch the ceremony. In the celestial skies of Heaven a host of angels gather for the Coronation. The Virgin humbly kneels, and bows her head to receive the Crown. The angels, dressed in a variety of colourful full length tunics and feathery long wings, watch and sing whilst it is placed upon her head, witnesses to a final acclamation of the purity of the Virgin and her place in religious history.

Ghirlandaio and Botticelli were both Italian painters of the Florentine school. Ghirlandaio is recognized for his masterly depiction of mass gatherings, as depicted here; Botticelli for his mastery of refined, courtly art.

Madonna and Child amongst the Saints Gregory and Nicholas, c. 1518
by Domenico Alfani (di Paride) (1479/80–1549/57)

The Virgin sits on a classical throne with her feet resting on steps beneath it. The infant Jesus is standing on her lap, his arms around her neck. She holds him closely to her with her right arm. Saints Gregory and Nicholas stand either side; their crowns are placed on the steps of the throne. In the background is the Umbrian countryside, placing the occasion in the artist's homeland. Above the throne, to either side two winged angels in colourful gowns hover horizontally, in mirror image. They carry a golden crown in their hands and together they are holding it, like a halo above the head of the Virgin. Their full length costumes and feathery wings are ruffled by the wind, creating movement within the setting. Angels, as the messengers of God, are confirming the Virgin as the Holy mother.

Domenico Alfani was a pupil of Perugino (1445–1523) and a friend of Raphael (1483–1520). The painterly style of Perugino and Raphael's work in the High Renaissance can be seen to influence this beautiful depiction of the Virgin and Child with Saints, which was painted for the church of S. Gregoria della Sapienza, in Perugia, Umbria. It bears resemblance to Raphael's *Virgin and Child* (the *Orléans Madonna*), c. 1506–07.

The Coronation of the Virgin, c. 1607
by Guido Reni (1575–1642)

Traditionally the Coronation of the Virgin is the final episode in the cycle of pictures glorifying Mary. Like the others it had no clear basis in the Scriptures, but this did not prevent it from becoming an extremely popular theme. Normally the Virgin is crowned by God the Father or Christ, but in Reni's picture (as in Alfani's – *see page 63*) two angels perform this task. Equally, she is frequently shown in regal attire, to emphasize her new status as 'the Queen of Heaven'. However, the real innovation in Reni's painting is the viewpoint. The spectator is given a ringside seat to the coronation, so close that the angel on the right turns round and looks over his shoulder, aware of the intrusion. The picture is also remarkable for the sheer variety of angels that are depicted. One of the oldest debates in this field is the thorny question of an angel's gender. Are they female, male, or sexless? Reni gave no definitive answer to this, though the two angels displayed prominently in the foreground are clearly male (right) and female (left).

Guido Reni (1575–1642) was a Bolognese painter, who produced much of his best work in Rome. He was hugely successful, maintaining a very large studio, and during his lifetime was ranked second only to Raphael.

The Dormition and Assumption of the Virgin, c. 1430
by Fra Angelico (c. 1395–1455)

This is an unusual combination of two popular themes glorifying the Virgin Mary. The Dormition (literally 'the Falling Asleep') refers to an old tradition that the Virgin did not die, but was actually in a deep sleep, during the three days which preceded her resurrection. As a composition, there are many similarities with The Death of the Virgin, which was a much more common theme in the West. In both cases, the Virgin is lying on her bed or a bier, surrounded by the apostles, who were miraculously assembled from various parts of the globe, in order to witness the scene. The Dormition was rarely depicted in the West, but it was a popular subject for the icon painters of the Eastern Church. Indeed, the Dormition itself was a major festival, celebrated on 15 August, and many churches were dedicated to it. The icon painters also introduced a few refinements of the theme. In some versions, Christ was present at the Virgin's side and carried off her soul himself. This was wrapped in swaddling clothes, like a newborn baby. The remainder of Fra Angelico's altarpiece is far more conventional, with the Virgin now in heaven, surrounded by a company of adoring angels.

The Assumption of the Virgin, c. 1474–76
by Francesco Botticini (c. 1446–98)

Patrons were often keen to personalize the religious pictures they commissioned, and there can be no more curious example of this than Botticini's unconventional rendering of *The Assumption of the Virgin*. The patron in question was Matteo Palmieri, a government officer who can be seen kneeling on the left. His widow is kneeling on the far side, dressed in the habit of a Benedictine nun. The Virgin's tomb, filled with her symbolic lilies, is set between them, while in the background, amidst a rolling landscape, Florence and Fiesole can be identified. A farm belonging to the donor is also included in the scene.

Palmieri had unusual religious views, some of which were later deemed to be heretical. Among other things, he believed that human souls could be equated with those angels who had remained neutral, when Satan waged his war against heaven. In this picture, he is also thought to be responsible for the highly questionable decision to introduce prophets and saints into the ranks of angels. Palmieri commissioned the picture for the altar in the burial chapel of San Pier Maggiore, in Florence. It is now in the National Gallery, in London.

Assumption of the Virgin, c. 1510
by Pinturicchio (c. 1454–1513)

The Assumption of the Virgin (literally 'the taking up of the Virgin') became an extremely popular subject in Western art, even though it has no firm Scriptural basis. Instead, the earliest accounts appeared in various apocryphal texts, dating from the fourth or fifth century. From an artistic point of view, however, it was the publication of the *Golden Legend*, which stimulated renewed interest in the subject. It also coincided with a growing cult of the Virgin, which increased the demand for subjects of this kind.

Pinturicchio's version of the theme shows the apostles, gathered at Mary's tomb. They watch in wonder as a group of angels bear her aloft, carrying her up to heaven. Mary is portrayed within a mandorla, an almond-shaped frame, adorned with angel heads. This is a larger alternative to a halo. It was originally employed in portrayals of Christ's Resurrection, although its use was gradually extended to other subjects, such as the Transfiguration. The inclusion of the angels is an essential feature of an *Assumption*. They emphasize that she was carried up to heaven, in contrast to Christ's Ascension, where He rose up of His own volition.

The Immaculate Conception
by the Circle of Juan de Valdés Leal (1622–90)

Comparable in many ways to the Assumption of the Virgin, the Immaculate Conception was another subject which glorified Mary's role. In its most widely found form, it developed during the Counter Reformation and reached the peak of its popularity in seventeenth-century Spain. The Immaculate Conception does not relate directly to the birth of Christ, but is concerned with the absolute purity of Mary herself. For doctrinal reasons, it was vital that she should be free from any taint of original sin. In 1854, the Immaculate Conception was promoted as an article of faith by Pope Pius IX.

In most versions of the subject, the Virgin is portrayed amongst the clouds, surrounded by angels, as in an *Assumption*. The most common identifying feature is an upturned crescent moon, an ancient symbol of chastity, placed beneath her feet. The theme was amplified by a series of emblems, most of which were drawn from the medieval Litanies of the Virgin. Here, for example, they include the ship, the tower, and the fountain, as well as the mirror carried by one of the angels.

Assumption of the Virgin, *c.* 1874
by Giuseppe Ghedine (*c.* 1823–94)

The Assumption of the Virgin Mary into heaven, which is said to have taken place three days after her death, is not mentioned in the Bible. However, it is an important part of Roman Catholic doctrine. The feast of the Assumption, celebrated each year on 15 August, is a public holiday in many countries where Catholicism is the dominant religion.

In this image of the *Assumption of the Virgin*, Mary appears to be travelling up a wide vertical shaft towards the golden light of heaven to be reunited with her Son and crowned the Queen of Heaven, signified by the blue of her robe. The use of aerial perspective, where the background becomes mistier and less distinct towards the top of the painting, creates a sense of distance and contrasts with the bolder figure of Mary, suggesting that she is floating in space.

This vertical shaft is lined with rings of cloud, stacked one above the other. These clouds appear like balconies or theatre boxes, and are populated with choirs of angels, singing and guiding Mary upwards towards heaven. She is borne aloft just above a bank of milk-white cloud on which cherubs tumble and play, reminding the viewer of Mary's purity and innocence.

CRUCIFIXION AND RESURRECTION

In most cases artists and patrons preferred to base their devotional pictures as closely as possible on the Scriptures. Occasionally however, extra details were added, to illustrate a point of doctrine. From the late Middle Ages, scenes of The Crucifixion often included angels collecting the blood from Christ's wounds. This was designed to emphasize the link between Christ's sacrifice and the Eucharist. An angel might also be shown retrieving the soul of the good thief, though he sometimes had to battle with a demon in order to achieve this.

Angels were not particularly common in Western depictions of the Entombment, but they were an ever-present feature of Eastern versions of the theme. The subject was often portrayed on ceremonial shrouds, which were placed on the altars of Orthodox churches during Easter week, to symbolize Christ's winding sheet. In these images, angels cluster around the body of Christ, holding *rhipidia* (liturgical fans), as emblems of the seraphim that worship around God's throne.

Depictions of the Resurrection sometimes included angels, although this subject was always slightly controversial, as it was not described in the gospels. Instead artists preferred to portray the angels who greeted Christ's friends, when they came to the empty sepulchre.

THE LAMENTATION, c. 1305–06
BY GIOTTO DI BONDONE (c. 1267–1337)

It is hard to believe that this painting was produced just 20 years or so after Duccio's *Rucellai Madonna* (*see* page 56). The artistic approach could scarcely be more different. Where the earlier picture is notable for its austere symbolism, Giotto's overflows with raw, human emotion. Nowhere is this more evident than in the treatment of the angels, who echo the sorrow of Christ's friends and family. Some of them wring their hands in despair, one buries its head in its gown, while another thrusts itself upwards, unable to look upon the tragic scene below. It is unusual to see depictions of angels showing this degree of physical emotion, even in scenes relating to the Crucifixion, but it certainly endows the picture with an added sense of poignant intensity.

Giotto displayed equal mastery in his depiction of the angels' forms. In most religious pictures these divine beings were portrayed as variants of humans, either with the addition of wings or painted on a different scale. Giotto, however, managed to convey the incorporeal nature of angels. Their heads and bodies may appear well defined, but they have no feet and even the hems of their garments seem to melt away into the sky.

CRUCIFIXION AND RESURRECTION

In most cases artists and patrons preferred to base their devotional pictures as closely as possible on the Scriptures. Occasionally however, extra details were added, to illustrate a point of doctrine. From the late Middle Ages, scenes of The Crucifixion often included angels collecting the blood from Christ's wounds. This was designed to emphasize the link between Christ's sacrifice and the Eucharist. An angel might also be shown retrieving the soul of the good thief, though he sometimes had to battle with a demon in order to achieve this.

Angels were not particularly common in Western depictions of the Entombment, but they were an ever-present feature of Eastern versions of the theme. The subject was often portrayed on ceremonial shrouds, which were placed on the altars of Orthodox churches during Easter week, to symbolize Christ's winding sheet. In these images, angels cluster around the body of Christ, holding *rhipidia* (liturgical fans), as emblems of the seraphim that worship around God's throne.

Depictions of the Resurrection sometimes included angels, although this subject was always slightly controversial, as it was not described in the gospels. Instead artists preferred to portray the angels who greeted Christ's friends, when they came to the empty sepulchre.

The LAMENTATION, c. 1305—06
by Giotto di Bondone (c. 1267—1337)

It is hard to believe that this painting was produced just 20 years or so after Duccio's *Rucellai Madonna* (*see* page 56). The artistic approach could scarcely be more different. Where the earlier picture is notable for its austere symbolism, Giotto's overflows with raw, human emotion. Nowhere is this more evident than in the treatment of the angels, who echo the sorrow of Christ's friends and family. Some of them wring their hands in despair, one buries its head in its gown, while another thrusts itself upwards, unable to look upon the tragic scene below. It is unusual to see depictions of angels showing this degree of physical emotion, even in scenes relating to the Crucifixion, but it certainly endows the picture with an added sense of poignant intensity.

Giotto displayed equal mastery in his depiction of the angels' forms. In most religious pictures these divine beings were portrayed as variants of humans, either with the addition of wings or painted on a different scale. Giotto, however, managed to convey the incorporeal nature of angels. Their heads and bodies may appear well defined, but they have no feet and even the hems of their garments seem to melt away into the sky.

The Crucifixion, fourteenth century
by Taddeo Gaddi (d. 1366)

Throughout the later Middle Ages and the Renaissance, artists often included angels in pictures of the Crucifixion. In many cases they carry tiny chalices, to collect the blood that spills from Christ's wounds. There were sound, doctrinal reasons for this, emphasizing the crucial link between Christ's sacrifice and the ritual of taking Holy Communion. Three of the angels in this scene gather blood, while the two at the top stretch out their arms, echoing Christ's pose on the Cross. The remaining angel turns away from the scene, unable to look at His suffering. This motif is reminiscent of Giotto's *Lamentation* (*see* pages 72–73), which is hardly surprising, since Gaddi was Giotto's godson.

The task of collecting Christ's blood was not always carried out by angels. The wound in His side was made by a Roman soldier called Longinus who, traditionally, is also identified as the centurion who declared: 'Truly, this man was a son of God'. With this in mind, he was sometimes depicted at the Crucifixion, holding out a sacred vessel to catch the drops of blood falling from the lance-wound. He is said to have taken this precious relic back to Mantua, eventually becoming the city's patron saint.

Trinity with Christ Crucified, c. 1410
by an unknown Austrian artist

Two angels are at the scene of a portrayal of *Trinity with Christ Crucified*, recognized as a 'Throne of Mercy' depiction. The Trinity are visible as Christ on the Cross, held by God the Father with the Holy Spirit, in the form of a dove, which flies between them. The youthful angels with pale skin and bright curly hair, kneel on the throne either side of God the Father. Their heads are bowed in prayer and their faces hold expressions of piety at the scene of Christ crucified. Each is dressed in long robes of complementary red and green, with gold decoration, a colour theme used throughout the work. The artist has given each angel complementary colour wings: red with green; green with red, to balance the illustration. Winged angels as attendants of God were depicted in religious paintings of Christ's birth, death and resurrection.

This is an Austrian work of the early fifteenth century, in egg tempera on wooden panel. It was possibly part of a portable altarpiece, as it originally was enclosed by two wooden doors to protect it. The depiction of angels with hands placed together in prayer replicate the actions of the owner of the altarpiece in daily prayer.

CRUCIFIXION OF JESUS CHRIST (detail), 1497–1522
by Pellegrino da San Daniele (1467–1547)

At the crucifixion of Christ two winged cherubim – recognized by their lack of bodies and their red and golden wings, fly to attend Christ, as he dies triumphant, on the Cross. Each angel carries a communion cup and holds it to catch the Blood of Christ. One holds the cup under the blood that spurts from Christ's nailed hand, the other to collect blood that spurts from the open wound in his side, caused by the Roman soldier's spear or sword. The Blood of Christ is a precious symbol of his suffering, in the Christian church, and symbolically drunk, in the form of wine, at communion.

Pellegrino (also known as Martino da Udine), was an Italian artist whose major work is in the church of San Antonio Abate in San Daniele, Friuli. The detail here is from his fresco masterpiece in the Church. Its naturalism in the rendition of Christ's life has led the work to be called the 'Sistine Chapel of Friuli'. The style of the work is typical of the High Renaissance paintings of the late-fifteenth century. The interest in Humanism, whereby mortals are a reflection of God, makes Jesus one like his people: human in body and suffering.

CRUCIFIED CHRIST WITH THE VIRGIN MARY, SAINTS AND ANGELS, c. 1502–03
by Raphael (1483–1520)

In this early painting by Raphael, which is also known as the *Mond Crucifixion* or *The Gavari Altarpiece*, two angels balance on tiptoe on thin slivers of cloud to collect the blood of Christ from the wounds in his hands and side. The painting was commissioned as an altarpiece for the funerary chapel of Domenico Gavari in Città di Castello in the Umbrian region of Italy, which he endowed so that masses could be said for his soul. The chalice-like shape of the vessels held by the angels remind those praying for the deceased's soul that the communion wine represents Christ's blood.

The angels in this painting are decorative and stylized, typical of Raphael's very earliest work. They appear flat compared to the more solid forms of the figures below, and their sashes swirl around them like calligraphic flourishes. Raphael's depiction of them may owe something to northern European images of angels and shows the influence of his father (the artist Giovanni Santi) and Perugino, to whom Raphael may have been apprenticed.

To balance the presence of the sun and moon at the top of the painting, which perhaps suggest the disruption of the cycle of night and day when Christ died, one angel wears dark clothing and the other pale.

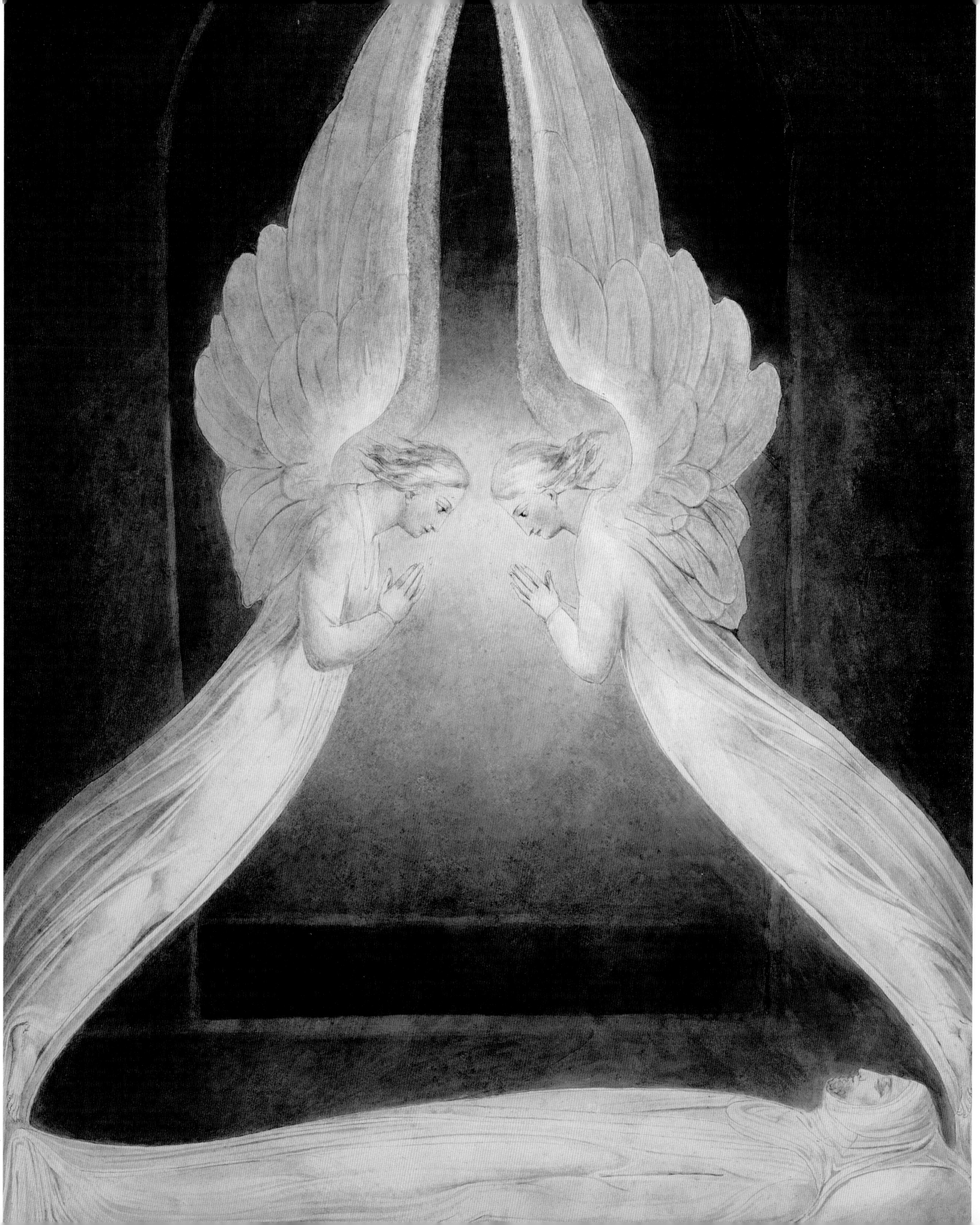

Christ in the Sepulchre, Guarded by Angels, *c.* 1805
by William Blake (1757–1827)

This striking image comes from a series of about 80 watercolours of Biblical scenes, which Blake produced for one of his chief patrons, Thomas Butts (1757–1845). At first glance it appears to depict a scene from the Gospels, although when Mary Magdalene saw the angels in Christ's sepulchre, His body had already gone (John 20:12). In fact Blake left a note below the image, showing that he drew his inspiration from a passage in the Old Testament (Exodus 25:18–20), describing the construction of a 'mercy seat' in the tabernacle: 'And thou shalt make two cherubims of gold … And the cherubims shall stretch forth their wings on high, covering the mercy seat with their wings, and their faces shall look one to another'. This passage was clearly meant to prefigure the New Testament scene, where the angels also sat at either end of the sepulchre, 'the one at the head and the other at the feet, where the body of Jesus had lain'.

The watercolour was shown at the Royal Academy (1808), as well as Blake's own exhibition (1809–10). It was one of the artist's favourite designs, and he expressed his desire to create a larger version of it, to serve as an altarpiece.

The Adoration of the Lamb (detail), completed 1432
by Jan and Hubert van Eyck (*c.* 1390–1441)

This is a detail of the main panel in *The Ghent Altarpiece*. In essence it is a celebration of the Eucharist, a symbol of Christ's sacrifice. On the front of the altar there is a quotation from the Gospels: 'Behold the Lamb of God, which taketh away the sin of the world' (John 1:29). Meanwhile the blood of the Lamb pours out into a communion chalice. The overall scene was probably inspired by a passage from Revelations (Rev. 7:9–17).

The angels grouped around the altar lead the way in worshipping the Lamb. Some have their hands clasped in prayer while others, kneeling behind the altar, display the Instruments of the Passion. These include the crown of thorns, the cross itself, the lance, the sponge of vinegar, and the pillar (a symbol of the Flagellation, when Christ was bound to a pillar). In front of the

altar two angels swing censers (incense-burners). These may seem incongruous in the open air but, in Christian art, censers were sometimes used as emblems of prayer – the idea being that prayers, like incense smoke, were wafted up to heaven. This notion stemmed from the Book of Psalms (141:2):

> *As incense let my prayer be
> directed in thine eyes.*

The Resurrection of Christ, c. 1501–02
by Raphael (1483–1520)

This small painting of Christ's resurrection measures just 52 by 44 cm, suggesting it was for private devotion rather than public worship in a church. Painted before Raphael was 20, the painting is also known as the *Kinnaird*

Resurrection as it was formerly in the collection at Kinnaird Castle in Perthshire, Scotland. There has been some dispute about the authorship of this work, but the recent discovery of signed preparatory drawings has made attribution to Raphael more convincing.

As in the *Crucified Christ* (*see* page 77), painted slightly after this one, Raphael's love of balanced composition and harmony is clearly evident. Indeed, his desire for a symmetrical composition gives this early image a rather contrived look. Apart from the central figure of Christ, the foreground figures are depicted in pairs and their poses closely mirror each other, including the two stylised angels who point heavenward against the lowering sky of dawn. The angels are very similar to those in the *Crucified Christ* although those depicted here are rather more realistic and their sashes are modest by comparison. Raphael based the painting shown here on a *Resurrection*, now in the Vatican Museum, painted two or three years earlier by Perugino.

The Resurrection of Christ, c. 1690
by Giuseppe Maria Crespi (1665–1747)

Giuseppe Crespi creates a dramatic scenario for the biblical narrative of the Resurrection of Christ, where his triumphant assent generates fear in mortals on the Earth. They throw their bodies to the ground and shield their faces from the strident light emanating from the risen body of Christ. The angels above, accompanying Christ, appear shocked by the powerful force of Christ Triumphant leaving Earth towards Heaven. They turn their bodies to make way for him. The artist's energetic brushwork adds drama, particularly in his strong contrasts of light and dark. The serpentine *contraposto* shapes of the bodies of Christ and the angels add to the dynamic motion of the painting. It is a truly Baroque depiction with accentuated use of *chiaroscuro* to highlight Christ's earthly body striding heavenward. The spectator angle is from below the scene, placed on the ground looking upward. The winged angels, dressed in loose draperies, are depicted swirling upward, either side of Christ. They are there as personifications of God, to accompany his risen Son to the celestial Heavens.

Giuseppe Crespi was an Italian artist from Bologna, known particularly for religious and mythological depictions. He painted against the traditions of the academic school to create naturalistic paintings.

ANGEL OF THE LORD ANNOUNCING the RESURRECTION to the THREE MARIES at the SEPULCHRE, 1805
by BENJAMIN WEST (1738–1820)

This glorious winged angel, with a commanding presence, dominates the pictorial scene. His sudden and unexpected arrival is portrayed through his strident leg movements and flowing draperies. He hovers above the empty sepulchre of Christ, looking toward the three women gathered at the side of the tomb. These are the three Maries, or Holy Women, who are mentioned in the four Gospels of the New Testament. It narrates that they were the first to discover Christ's empty sepulchre. (Matthew 28:1–8; Mark 16:1–8; Luke 24: 1–11; John 20: 1–19). One perhaps may be Mary Magdalene. They stand near to the shocked and fearful Roman guards, who hold their shields to protect themselves whilst looking at the messenger from God. The angel, dressed in a luminous white drapery that barely covers his body, gestures with his right hand towards the empty tomb. His left arm is extended upward and his hand points heavenward, to gesture that Christ has risen to Heaven. The deeply coloured curls of the angel's hair contrast with his pale body. He is depicted larger than the mortals in the picture, a symbol of his heavenly status.

Benjamin West was an American history and portrait painter who studied in Italy, later moving to London, England.

Why Seek Ye the Living Among the Dead?, 1880s
by A.C. Lalli, after John Rodham Spencer Stanhope
(Stanhope 1829–1908)

This is a striking Victorian version of a theme that is usually known as
The Holy Women at the Sepulchre or The Three Maries at the Sepulchre.
It portrays the followers of Christ, who had been present at the Crucifixion
and had then gone home to prepare oils and spices so that they could
anoint the body. However, when they arrived at Christ's tomb early in the
morning, they discovered that He was no longer there.

Stanhope used a quotation from the gospel of Saint Luke as his title
(Luke 24:5), although he also ignored details from this gospel and those of
the other Evangelists. Luke and John, for example, specified that there were
two angels, but it suited the artist better to just show one. Luke also
mentioned that the angels were male ('two men in shining garments') but,
along with many other Victorian painters, Stanhope preferred to portray
angels as female.

The women have brought their unguents. One holds a jar of ointment,
while a casket of myrrh is placed by the angel's feet. The names of the
women varied from gospel to gospel, but Luke identified them as Mary
Magdalene, Joanna and Mary, the mother of James.

Archangel Michael

In Western art Michael is chiefly associated with two main roles. In his military guise, he is the captain of the heavenly host. At the start of time, he leads them in the fight against Satan and his rebel angels. Then, at the hour of the Second Coming, he leads them again, when 'there was war in heaven; Michael and his angels fought against the dragon ... and the great dragon was cast out, that old serpent called the Devil' (Revelations 12:7–9). In keeping with his martial prowess the archangel is frequently shown wearing armour and wielding a sword. During the Middle Ages several military orders were dedicated to his name.

Michael's other main function, inherited from the pagan gods of antiquity, is as a psychopomp, a conductor of souls to the afterlife. He is also responsible for weighing the souls of the dead at the time of the Last Judgement. With this in mind he is often portrayed holding a pair of scales.

In addition to these duties Michael is associated with several other roles. He is acclaimed as the champion of the Jewish people, while the Christians in Egypt regarded him as the protector of the Nile. In the East he is revered as a healer, and in Normandy as the patron of mariners.

Saint Michael, completed 1469
by Piero della Francesca (c. 1415–92)

Saint Michael, also known as Archangel Michael, is often shown trampling on the defeated devil in the form of a dragon or large serpent, symbolizing his victory over the powers of evil. In this work, Piero della Francesca depicts the decapitated serpent, whose head the saint holds in his left hand, as still writhing under his feet. Michael's wings are styled on those of a swan, suggesting purity.

Unusually for an angel, Michael is shown dressed in Roman armour, which is underscored by the classical architecture shown behind him, consisting of an entablature and Corinthian pilasters. This military attire symbolizes his role in the 'war in Heaven', mentioned in the Bible in Revelations. As a result of this, Saint Michael is patron saint of soldiers and policemen. His armour is, however, more lavish than that issued to mere mortals: close inspection reveals that it is studded with precious stones and pearls. He also wears an unusual gossamer-fine undergarment with jewelled cuffs and collar and tiny buttons on the sleeve.

This image was part of an altarpiece for Sant' Agostino in his home town of Sansepulcro. The altarpiece originally consisted of several panels each depicting different saints, although these are now dispersed in different collections.

Saint Michael, date unknown
by Bernardino Zenale (1436–1526)

Zenale's painting is a magnificent depiction of the multi-tasking saint, illustrating his two major roles. With his right hand, he thrusts his sword through the devil, fulfilling the prophecy in the Book of Revelation. With his left hand, meanwhile, he judges the souls of the dead by weighing them in a balance.

The concept of weighing souls was borrowed from pagan antiquity. It featured in the religious beliefs of the Egyptians, the Greeks and the Romans. Michael's association with it probably developed through his links with Mercury (*see* pages 182–84). There are also a number of Biblical passages that refer to the practice. The most famous of these occurred in the Old Testament, as part of the Belshazzar's warning: 'Thou art weighed in the balances, and art found wanting' (Daniel 5:27).

The depiction of Saint Michael with scales is most commonly found in paintings of the *Last Judgement*, when he is usually placed before God's throne. The scales traditionally contain two souls, one in either pan. As in Zenale's painting, the balance is uneven. The heavier soul is said to be the righteous one. In some versions of the scene, the devil tilts the scales, to upset the process. Zenale's stricken demon extends a claw, as if to attempt the same trick.

angel and contrasting with the beautiful feathered wings of his captor.

As with Piero della Francesca's *Saint Michael* (*see* page 86), Michael is depicted wearing Roman armour, although in this painting the artist offers a more fanciful interpretation with a gauze-like sash and cape, giving him an element of immateriality. Michael's blond hair, elegant pose and refined features could not be more at odds with the brutish features and solid flesh of Satan, who is chained like a wild beast. Michael gently holds the other end of the lead, showing that he is in control. Despite Satan's muscularity and apparent strength, Michael triumphs over his more powerful-looking enemy because he has righteousness on his side.

The diagonal composition of this image creates a powerful effect as the strong line from top left to bottom right prefigures the thrust his sword is about to take, leaving the resulting death-blow to our imagination.

Archangel Michael (detail of Madonna in Glory fresco at Santa Maria di Strada), sixteenth century
by an unknown artist

In this detail from the *Madonna in Glory* fresco in the Church of Santa Maria di Strada, a rampant Archangel Michael charges forth to protect the Madonna as she ascends to Heaven. His role is set as the 'prince of angels' and as such he is given a leading role on this ceremonial occasion. He wears a long red tunic tied with a flowing blue sash. His blue wings symbolize his dwelling place in heaven, as an attendant of God. The doctrine of the Blessed Virgin Mary decrees that when 'her earthly life was finished, [she] was taken body and soul into the glory of Heaven.' (The Assumption). This takes place on the third day after her death and religious scriptures tell that the Archangel Michael accompanies her body to Paradise. The biblical texts on the Assumption mention various malevolent characters trying to disrupt the proceedings. The Archangel Michael is on hand to repel all those with dishonest intent, and punish wrongdoers, as depicted here. A winged personification of Satan, with long claw nails, is cast out and tumbles downwards with Michael above him, armed with fiery sword. This work of the High Renaissance shows its mastery of perspective.

Saint Michael, 1635
after Guido Reni (1575–1642)

Here Archangel Michael tramples on the devil, this time in human form, rather than being depicted as a serpent or dragon, as is often the case. On closer inspection we see that this figure is not entirely human: he has dark, reptilian wings on his back, emphasizing his role as a fallen

Triumph of Saint Michael (sketch), c. 1830–48
by Eugène Delacroix (1798–1863)

The Archangel Saint Michael is the chief Angel and Prince of the Seraphim, whose name translates as 'he who is like to God'. His origins are considered to be in Persian culture. He is also linked to Hebrew sources, a guardian angel of their nation (Daniel: 10:13, 21). He was embraced by the Christian church and his fiery force against Evil is narrated in the Bible in the Book of Revelations: 12:7–9.

Eugène Delacroix, a French painter, writer and lithographer of the Romantic period, depicts an emotional, tumultuous scene. Saint Michael appears in triumph above what is probably a defeatd Satan and the aftermath of a struggle. The intense brushwork and remarkable use of colour accentuates the movement of Michael and the blustery formidable clouds of the sky. The imagery could have political undertones, considering Delacroix's involvement in the Revolution of 1830, in France.

Saint Michael, 1988–90
Yaroslav and Galina Dobrynine

This striking mural comes from the monastery of Saint-Antoine-le-Grand, which nestles in a picturesque valley, in the Vercors region of south-eastern France. Founded in 1978, this is a Greek Orthodox church, a dependant of the famous monastery on Mount Athos. The interior is sumptuously decorated with a series of frescoes and icons. Most of the work was carried out by Yaroslav Dobrynine and his wife, Galina. Together, they covered over 600 square metres with their wall-paintings. The couple have considerable experience in this field, having already worked on churches in France, Palestine and Russia. One of their most high-profile projects was the decoration of the crypt in Saint Saviour's Cathedral in Moscow.

The style of the murals at Saint-Antoine-le-Grand is based very firmly on early Russian icons. Saint Michael is portrayed in his military guise, wearing his armour and wielding his sword. It is in this form that he will lead the angelic horde, in the final battle against Satan.

Devils and Rebel Angels

Angels Fighting Devils (detail from altarpiece), c. 1433
by Jaume Cirera

The cataclysmic battles between the heavenly host and Satan and his followers allowed artists to give full rein to their imagination. During these encounters the fallen angels could be shown in their original form, similar in many ways to the angels. This is certainly the line that artists such as William Blake and Gustave Doré took when they were illustrating scenes from Milton's *Paradise Lost*. In altarpieces, however, there was a greater tendency to turn them into demons, to emphasize that these conflicts represented a primal struggle between good and evil.

The satanic forms came from many sources. The more outlandish monsters were often inspired by Eastern prototypes. The Egyptians, Persians and Mesopotamians all portrayed creatures that were a blend of different animals. Artists also borrowed ideas from classical culture. Many traditional aspects of the devil – the tail, the cloven hooves, the horns, the goat-like features – were reminiscent of satyrs. These woodland creatures were not particularly evil, but they could be interpreted as symbols of a pagan past.

A Battle Triumphant is raging in this image of *Angels Fighting Devils*, from the Altarpiece of Saint Peter and Saint Michael. The Saints Peter and Michael are traditionally placed as the guardians of the Gates or Doors to Heaven. Here, in Heaven with God the Father on his Throne, a rampant battle is taking place between good and evil. Good angels are depicted with wings and golden haloes, and are armed with shields and swords, in the ascendant. The evil devils are climbing up toward Heaven from the fiery red furnace of Hell. The artist depicts devils as dark animalistic creatures with bat-like wings, tails and cloven feet. The mouth of hell has sharply jagged teeth.

The iconography of the painting would have needed no explanation to an onlooker. The story of the battle between good angels and devils, and the expulsion of Lucifer's band of rebels, is taken from various religious texts. Here, Saint Michael the Archangel, wearing a coat of armour, strikes at Lucifer, the Devil, with a long trident, seen here at centre left.

Fall of the Rebel Angels, fifthteenth century
by Guillermo Talarn

The battle between good angels, on the side of God, and rebels belonging to the Devil's band of dissidents, is taken from the Creation and Apocalypse narratives in religious texts. Traditional depictions show Archangel Michael and Saint Peter guarding God the Father, seated on a throne in Heaven. In this illustration the beautiful winged angels strike out with swords and shields to protect their heavenly Paradise. They have caught the Devil, seen at the centre of the battle. He is painted as half man-half beast, naked and wounded; a sword running through his scrawny body. He has two faces, one is horned and fights forward, and the other face is on his rear end and looks down toward Hell. His rebels are a motley bunch of creatures with animalistic attributes of four feet and cloven hooves. They pitch forth into the murky waters below, wingless angels of evil. The artist has painted a dramatic portrayal of the battle. One can see a four-legged rebel to the left clinging on to the shield of a good angel, to try to unbalance him; others with bloody wounds retreat or fall below.

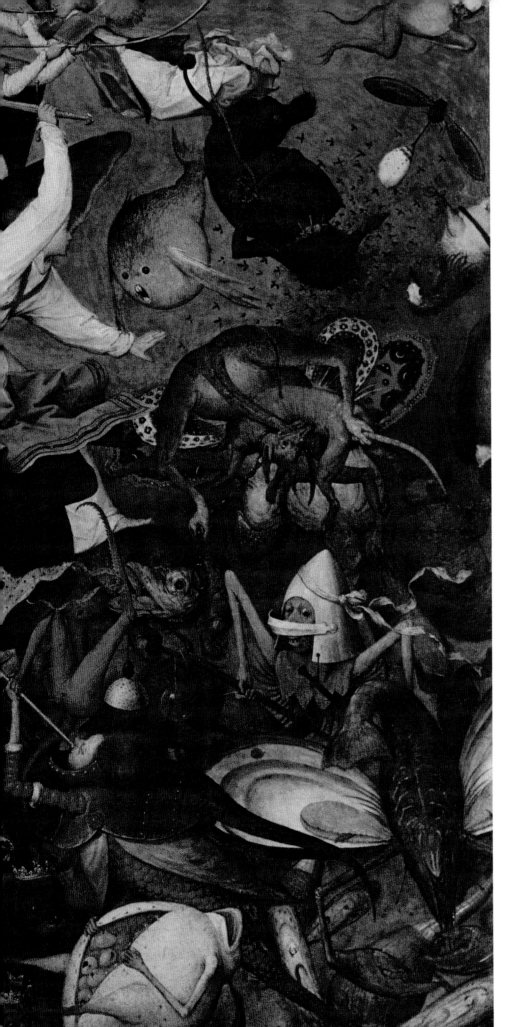

Fall of the Rebel Angels, 1562
by Pieter Bruegel the Elder (c. 1525–69)

Strictly speaking this subject occurred near the start of creation, before the emergence of humanity. However, it frequently became confused with scenes from the apocalypse, as described in the Book of Revelation. As usual, Saint Michael takes centre stage. With his suit of armour, he is easily distinguishable from the other warrior angels. The depiction of the fallen angels, on the other hand, varied considerably. When artists were illustrating *Paradise Lost*, for example, they frequently portrayed the fallen angels in human form, with or without wings, largely because they sounded so human in Milton's text. However, when the subject was portrayed in altarpieces and other religious pictures, Satan's followers were normally depicted as monsters. In some cases, artists showed this transformation taking place, with the vanquished losing their angelic form as they fell from heaven, sprouting fangs and tails.

Some painters gained considerable renown for their monsters. In the Netherlands, the most gruesome creatures were certainly produced by Hieronymus Bosch (*c.* 1450–1516) and Pieter Bruegel. In this picture, the fallen angels are overcome by their own vices. Some are crushed by giant musical instruments or outlandish pieces of food, while others still retain traces of their former selves. They have human heads, to blow their horns, but their arms are withered and their bodies have developed reptilian scales.

Satan Arousing the Rebel Angels, 1808
by William Blake (1757–1827)

Over the years Blake produced several series of illustrations for John Milton's (1608–74) epic poem, *Paradise Lost* (1667). This dramatic scene depicts a key episode from Book 1 (l.300–40). The rebel angels have been thrown out of heaven and are lying prostrate and dejected in the burning lake in Chaos. Some of them are still wearing manacles. Satan chides them for their defeatist attitude, crying 'Awake, arise, or be for ever fall'n'.

The depiction of Satan created a quandary for many artists. How could they show his angelic origins, while also stressing his demonic nature? Blake opted to portray him as a classical nude, inspired partly by antique statuary and partly by his favourite artist, Michelangelo (1475–1564). There are no wings and no tail, although in some scenes there is a serpent coiled around his torso. This is not particularly surprising as Blake's immediate source was Milton, rather than the Bible, and the poet endowed his villain with a certain grandeur. Nevertheless it meant that his portrayal of Satan and his minions was very different from the versions that appeared in traditional, religious paintings. The overall composition has been likened to a gloomy pastiche of the Resurrection, where the dead rise from their graves to face the Last Judgement.

Fall of the Rebel Angels, 1866
by Gustave Doré (1832–83)

This turbulent scene is one of a series of engravings that Doré produced for his edition of John Milton's (1608–74) *Paradise Lost*. It illustrates this passage:

> '…Him the Almighty Power
> Hurled headlong flaming from th' ethereal sky
> With hideous ruin and combustion down
> To bottomless perdition…'   (Book 1, 44–47)

Unlike many other treatments of this theme (*see* pages 94–95), Satan and his followers are portrayed in their angelic form. Even in the moment of their defeat, they still retain their wings, their weapons and their armour.

Angels featured very prominently in Doré's work. In addition to his Milton engravings, they can also be found in his editions of Dante's *Inferno* (1857), Michaud's *History of the Crusades* (1875), Samuel Taylor Coleridge's *Rime of the Ancient Mariner* (1870) and his final project, Edgar Allan Poe's *The Raven* (published posthumously in 1884). The appearance of Doré's angels was unexceptional, but he was particularly gifted at portraying them en masse.

Doré's art was hugely popular on both sides of the Channel. For more than 20 years he had a gallery in New Bond Street, in London, specializing in his work. This included religious paintings, though he has also become well known for his bleak depictions of the London slums.

HEAVEN AND JUDGEMENT

Angels obviously make a very significant appearance in pictures of the Last Judgement, as the momentous events take place against the backdrop of the Court of Heaven. In addition, several angels play an active part in the proceedings. Their first action is to raise the dead by sounding their trumpets. Then, as judgement begins, Michael comes to the fore, weighing human souls in his scales. After this, angels shepherd the souls away to their respective fates. Some are assisted into Paradise, while others are escorted to hell. They may be thrown down there physically by angels in armour, bearing swords.

In the East, icon painters produced an interesting variation on this theme. They portrayed the route to the afterlife as a heavenly ladder, stretching up to paradise. Some of the climbing figures were assisted by angels, while others were knocked off the ladder by demons. The image is reminiscent of the ladder in Jacob's dream (Genesis 28:12).

There were also a multitude of angels involved in the Apocalypse, a subject that was especially popular in Spain. Some worship around the throne of the Holy Lamb, while the terrible afflictions that rain down upon the world are heralded by seven angels, blowing their trumpets.

ETERNAL BLESSING, c. 1485–1523
by PIETRO VANNUCCI PERUGINO
(c. 1445–1523)

Pietro Vannucci Perugino of Perugia, Umbria, Italy, is noted for the sweet style and symmetrical balance revealed in the phenomenal amount of artworks he produced in his lifetime. He was a master of the High Renaissance in painting. In *Eternal Blessing*, a detail from a larger painting, God the Father is seated at the oval open portal to heaven, resting on a heavenly cloud and looking down to the scene below. He raises his right hand in a sign of eternal blessing. He is surrounded by winged seraphim and cherubim, the messengers and attendants of God. They are identified by their heads without bodies. They have three sets of wings, one at their face, one at the feet and one in flight. Seraphim are traditionally with red wings, to signify burning love; the cherubim have blue wings to signify their celestial home in heaven. The text from Isaiah (6:1–2) states: 'I saw the Lord seated... about him stood the seraphim; each had six wings: with two he covered his face, and with two he covered his feet, and with two he flew...' Pietro has literally depicted the bible narration in this charming scene. He is noted for the harmonious colours and beauty of his works, taken further by Raphael.

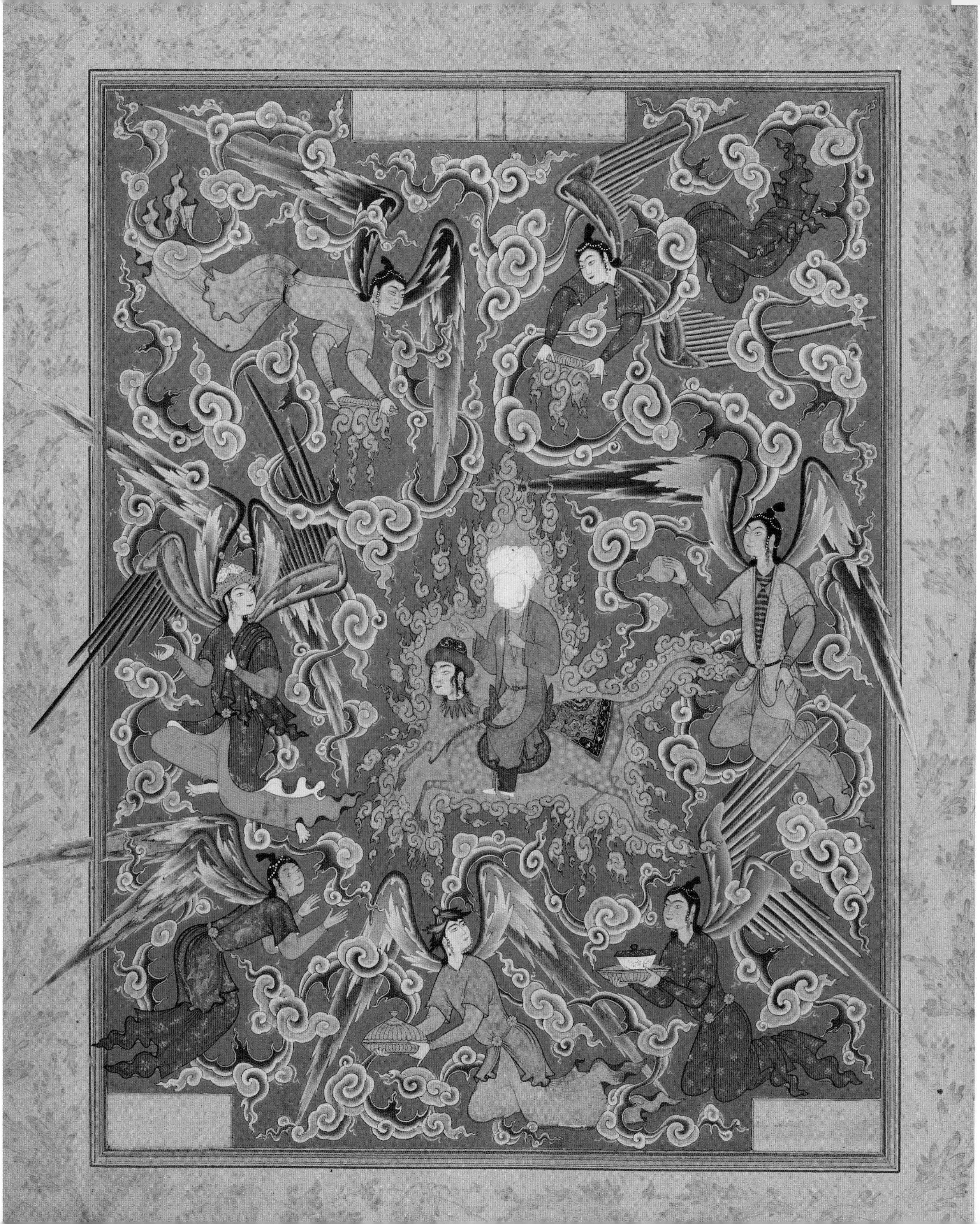

Ascent of the Prophet to Heaven, *c.* 1550
ascribed to Ja'far al-Sadiq, from a copy of the Falnama or Book of Omens

In this astonishingly bright and detailed Persian miniature, from the same book as the image on pages 22–23, we can see Muhammad riding to heaven astride the fabled Buraq, a horse-like creature from the heavens that is said to have the face of a woman, the feet and tail of a camel, and a saddle and bridle fashioned from jewels. The Buraq (from the Arabic word for lightning) is supposedly able to travel as far as the eye can see in just one bound and is sometimes depicted with the tail of a peacock.

In this image the Prophet's face is veiled – only his clothes are depicted. He and the Buraq are surrounded by sacred fire and by a host of brightly clad angels, dressed in the courtly clothes of the time and endowed with huge angular wings. These heavenly beings attend to Muhammad, showing him the way and beckoning him towards Paradise. Stylized clouds around the angels give the image a remarkable patterned quality and act as a veil between earth and heaven.

Persian artists used high-quality pigments ground from the most costly materials, resulting in beautiful, bright colours that have not lost their richness in over 450 years.

The Death of the Good Old Man, 1808
by William Blake (1757–1827)
(engraved by Louis Schiavonetti)

William Blake was, quite literally, a visionary artist, and his mystic experiences had a major impact on his art. At the age of ten he claimed to have seen a company of angels sitting in a tree, 'bespangling every bough like stars'. On another occasion he sensed a group of angelic spirits walking amongst some haymakers. These apparitions inspired both his writings and his art. In his books he described his 'memorable fancies', when he dined with prophets and conversed with archangels, while in his watercolours he portrayed his own, very personal cosmology. This led him to create startlingly different versions of angelic forms. He portrayed God, for example, as an old man with luxuriant wings, and showed cherubims riding on horseback.

This picture is one of a series of illustrations, which Blake produced for Robert Blair's poem, 'The Grave' (*see* page 102). It formed an obvious pair with another of his designs, *The Death of the Strong Wicked Man*, where the soul of the deceased is wrenched away from its body in a fiery torment. In this instance the lower half of the composition, with the corpse and the kneeling mourners, was inspired by the drawings of tomb effigies, which Blake produced during his days as an apprentice.

The Meeting of a Family in Heaven, 1808
by William Blake (1757–1827) (engraved by Louis Schiavonetti)

Blake was an extraordinarily versatile artist who managed to excel in a number of different fields. He produced some of his most imaginative designs for book illustrations. This particular image was created for a de luxe edition of 'The Grave', a lengthy poem by the Scottish clergyman Robert Blair (1699–1746). First published in 1743, this was probably the best known work by a member of the 'graveyard poets', and its gloomy subject matter provided ideal material for Blake's fevered imagination. Despite this, the project was beset with problems. In 1805, the publisher Robert Cromek commissioned Blake to produce 40 watercolours based on the text, on the understanding that he would later be asked to engrave the best of these for the book. However, Cromek changed his mind and passed the job across to Louis Schiavonetti. His lifeless engravings do little justice to Blake's watercolours.

Blake's designs owe much to his apprenticeship days when he copied the tomb sculptures in Westminster Abbey. This left him with a fondness for Gothic details. He employed this formation of angels several times (*see* page 78), using the curve of their wings to form a Gothic arch over his figures.

The Soul of the Penitent Thief, c. 1886–94
by James Tissot (1836–1902)

In common with *The Annunciation* (*see* page 45), this painting was produced as part of Tissot's ambitious scheme to provide a comprehensive series of illustrations of Christ's life. This particular scene relates to an episode from the Crucifixion. Jesus was crucified between two thieves, one of whom mocked the Saviour, while the other repented of his sins. Christ comforted the latter, promising him that 'Today you shall be with me in Paradise'.

In contrast to Tissot's version, most artists set this subject at the time of the Crucifixion, while the dead bodies of the thieves were still attached to their crosses. By focusing instead on the thief's celestial journey Tissot introduced a number of different features. Earlier painters usually visualized heaven as a haven of golden light, situated above the clouds, but the thief's posthumous flight takes him into a starry night, perhaps even into outer space. He is accompanied by dozens of other angels, each presumably carrying a similar cargo. The angels themselves are seraphims, identifiable from their six wings as described in the Book of Isaiah.

Angels welcoming the Saved into Paradise, 1896
by William Morris (1834–96)

When most Christian artists portrayed the souls of the righteous arriving in the afterlife, they tended to visualize heaven as an airy domain, high above the sky. This idea held no attraction for William Morris, who much preferred the notion of an earthly Paradise. His figures, in fact, are returning to the Garden of Eden. As in his *Adam and Eve* (*see* page 28), this has a deliberately archaic flavour. The boundary takes the form of a castle wall, while one of the angels is holding a medieval musical instrument.

This illustration comes from the Kelmscott *Chaucer*, the most lavish of all the books produced at Morris's private press. The project took five years to complete because, as usual, he was insistent that every aspect of the production should be perfect. He designed a special new typeface for the book and spared no effort in finding the right kind of handmade paper and inks. This led to so many delays that one of his books was dubbed 'the interminable' by his workers at the press. Morris was dying by the time that the *Chaucer* was finished, but he lived to see the very first copy. He noted this in his diary, with the comment 'Very satisfactory'.

Apocalypse, fifthteenth century
Flemish manuscript illumination by an unknown artist

The Apocalypse is the final day of Judgement according to the Holy Scriptures. On that day according to The Revelations of St John, the last book of the bible, everyone will be judged. The artist has depicted symbols and personifications of the apocalypse, which would have been easily recognized by a Christian worshipper. The scripture (Revelations 4–5) writes that '…in heaven a door had opened', which is depicted by a tall winged angel pulling apart an opening into heaven, '…one seated on a throne… on each side of the throne are four living creatures …a lion, an ox, the face of a man and a flying eagle.' The text reveals that each creature will have six wings. Also present would be seraphim and cherubim, attendants of God. They were illustrated as winged heads without bodies. The seraph traditionally has red wings; the cherub has blue wings. The seven torches of fire, as seven spirits of God are depicted above the throne. In the background twenty four elders fall down and worship 'him who lives forever', and cast their crowns before the throne. The artist has achieved much of this in this illustration, which probably illuminated the appropriate text in Revelations.

Last Judgement, 1432–35
by Fra Angelico (*c.* 1395–1455)

The Last Judgement occurs at the end of time, following the Second Coming of Christ. Angels sound the last trump and the dead rise from their graves. This has already happened in Fra Angelico's painting, where the centre of the composition is dominated by two rows of empty tombs. In many versions, the dead are shown clambering out of their graves. Occasionally they are portrayed as skeletons undergoing a transformation, turning back to flesh and blood.

Christ sits in majesty at the pinnacle of the composition, surrounded by angels. The judging process was described in many parts of the Bible, most notably in Matthew: 'And before him shall be gathered all nations; and he shall separate them one from another, as a shepherd divideth his sheep from the goats; And he shall set the sheep on his right hand, but the goats on the left' (Matthew 25:32–33). Fra Angelico has depicted this on the sides of his picture (as shown below), with the saved forming a circle in Paradise, while the 'goats' are led away to the torments of hell.

This painting, along with many others, is now housed at the San Marco Museum in Florence. This was once a monastery, where Fra Angelico produced some of his finest work, but it has now been turned into a showcase for the artist.

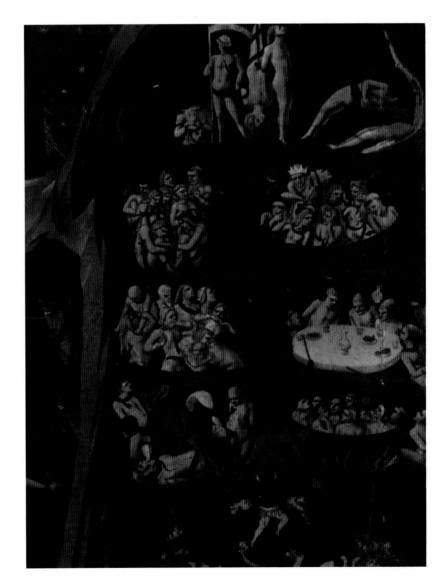

Christ the Judge, 1447
by Fra Angelico (Giovanni da Fiesole) (c. 1387–1455)

Christ the Judge by Fra Angelico is part of a ceiling fresco in the vault of La Cappella della Madonna di San Brizio (the chapel of the Madonna of San Brizio) in Orvieto Cathedral, Umbria, Italy. Fra Angelico is renowned for his deeply moving portrayals of biblical narrative. Here the Risen Christ sits in judgement of mortals. He is seated and held aloft on a throne of clouds. A celestial throng of youthful, winged angels with golden haloes kneel on clouds either side of him. They are dressed in identical long garments in two colours. The garment collars are trimmed with gold. Some are shown in profile to reveal their long slim wings. The angels look towards the heavens, towards Christ, towards the multitude below and out and towards the spectator.

Fra Angelico was a devout monk of the Dominican fraternity and an outstanding artist. He took his style from fourteenth-century Gothic paintings, which can be seen in his use of angels in profile, the background in gold and decorative gold touches to Christ and the Angels' haloes and clothing. The work was finished by Luca Signorelli (c. 1441–1523).

The Calling of the Elect into Heaven, c. 1499–1502
by Luca Signorelli (c. 1441–1523)

Paintings of the Last Judgement were usually conceived as one vast scene, designed to impress any congregation. However, it was equally possible to break the subject down into its component parts. This was the approach adopted by Luca Signorelli in his masterpiece, the cycle of frescoes in the San Brizio Chapel in Orvieto Cathedral.

Signorelli's cycle consisted of several major scenes, among them *The Preaching of the Antichrist*, *The Destruction of the World*, *The Resurrection of the Flesh*, *The Calling of the Elect into Heaven*, and *The Damned Consigned to Hell*. Most of these compositions were constructed in a similar manner. At the top of the picture, framed by an arch, there was a group of large angels, while below there was a dense crowd of smaller, human figures. In this picture, heaven is represented by a celestial orchestra, while other angels help the saved to ascend to their new home. In *The Resurrection*, by contrast, the upper section is devoted to two muscular, male angels, sounding the last trump, accompanied by a group of tiny putti.

Saints and Angels

Saints were often included in devotional pictures of the Virgin and Child with angels. In most cases, they were featured because of some link with the commission. The saint in question might be the namesake of the patron, or of the church where the picture was to hang. In many examples the saint and the donor might be placed on a side-panel, though they could also be shown participating in the sacred event. It was not unusual, for example, to find them included in a scene like the *Assumption of the Virgin* (*see* pages 66–67). This type of picture is sometimes known as a *Sacra Conversazione* ('Sacred Conversation').

Of all the saints, angels are probably most commonly found with John the Baptist. He was frequently portrayed in pictures of the Holy Family, where both he and Christ were depicted as infants. In Eastern icons, John himself was sometimes portrayed with wings, as the 'Angel of the Desert'. The idea here was to emphasize how John, like Gabriel, was a messenger heralding the arrival of Jesus. Many saints had individual encounters with angels. Sometimes the latter were offering them assistance, in their hour of need. At other times they appeared to the saint in a vision, bringing them tidings from the Lord.

Saint Matthew in Bishop More's Book of Prayers, eighth century
by an unknown artist

Portraits of the four Evangelists were a regular feature of early Celtic manuscripts such as this. The pictures and the ornamental lettering were extremely useful to clerics, helping them to find their way around a Biblical text that, as yet, had not been divided into chapters and verses. The figures of the Evangelists were inspired by the author portraits in classical manuscripts, but their identifying symbols were an innovation. According to this convention, Matthew was represented by a winged man, Mark by a lion, Luke by an ox, and John by an eagle.

These symbols were mentioned in a prophecy by Ezekiel (1:10), but stemmed ultimately from the apocalyptic beasts worshipping at God's feet in Revelations: '...and round about the throne were four beasts, full of eyes before and behind. And the first beast was like a lion, and the second beast like a calf, and the third beast had a face as a man...' (Rev. 4:6–9). The validity of these symbols was confirmed by Saint Jerome (342–420) and accepted by the Church. Technically Matthew's emblem is not an angel, though it was often represented as such. However, some artists interpreted the man as a cleric and depicted the symbol as an angel with a priest's tonsure.

The Liberation of Saint Peter (detail), 1513–14
by Raphael (1483–1520)

Peter's miraculous escape from prison is described in the New Testament (Acts 12:1–11). During Herod's persecution of the Christians in Rome the apostle was one of those placed under arrest. By night, however, the angel of the Lord entered the prison in a burst of radiant light and found Peter sleeping between two guards. He roused the saint and touched his chains, which immediately fell to the ground. Then the angel led Peter away, out of the jail and as far as the city gates.

The subject is relatively unusual, but this version is widely regarded as a major highlight of Raphael's greatest undertaking – a cycle of frescoes decorating the papal apartments in the Vatican. He was commissioned by Pope Julius II, who chose this subject specifically for one of the most impressive chambers, the Stanza d'Eliodoro. It was designed to commemorate a recent victory over a French invasion force, which was repelled in 1512. On the eve of the invasion the Pope had gone to pray in the church where he had once been a cardinal, San Pietro in Vincoli (literally 'Saint Peter in Chains'). This church had gained its unusual name because, amongst its relics, it claimed to own the very shackles that Saint Peter wore in prison.

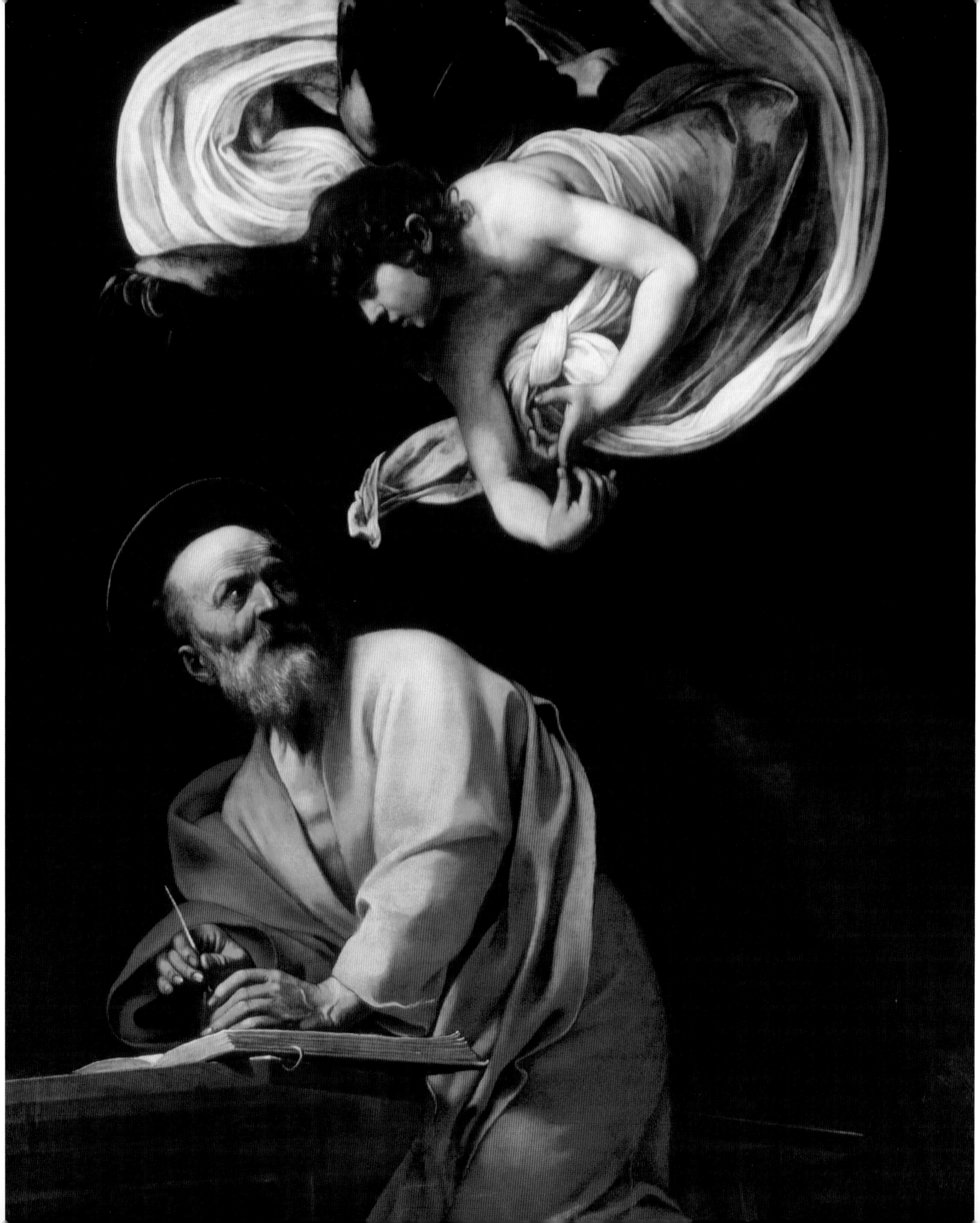

Saint Matthew and the Angel, 1602
by Michelangelo Merisi da Caravaggio (1571–1610)

Also known as *The Inspiration of Saint Matthew*, this picture illustrates the old tradition that the Evangelist wrote his gospel with divine assistance. Caravaggio has portrayed this in a very literal fashion. While the saint is sitting at his table, working on his text, an angel swoops down to offer advice, counting the points off on his fingers.

This painting formed part of Caravaggio's first major commission. In 1599 he was hired to decorate the Contarelli Chapel, in the church of San Luigi dei Francesi in Rome. The patron wanted scenes from the life of his namesake, Saint Matthew, and the artist duly produced three paintings. This particular subject, however, proved controversial. Caravaggio had developed a taste for depicting religious themes with a brutal sense of realism, but his first version of *Saint Matthew and the Angel* went too far and was rejected. It made the Evangelist seem like a simpleton, with the angel guiding his hands, to form the words of the gospel. This version was deemed acceptable, although the saint's undignified pose and his bare feet still attracted some criticism.

Saint Sebastian attended by Angels, 1602–03
by Peter Paul Rubens (1577–1640)

In artistic terms, Sebastian is one of the most instantly recognizable saints. Almost always, painters showed him bound to a pillar or a tree, with a number of arrows piercing his body. Sometimes the archers were also depicted, firing their weapons at their helpless victim. Rubens' composition, with its group of ministering angels, is an unusual variant of the subject.

In reality, virtually nothing is known about Sebastian, other than that he was a Roman martyr, who probably died in AD 286. According to legend, he was a high-ranking soldier, an officer in the Praetorian guard, who practised his faith in secret. When his beliefs were eventually discovered, however, he was condemned to death. The arrows of his executioners failed to kill him, though, and he was gradually restored to health by a Roman widow called Irene. She is now revered as the patron saint of nurses.

The earliest depictions of the saint portray him as a bearded man without his arrow wounds. His traditional image only became popular after worshippers began to invoke his name for protection against the plague. This stemmed from an old superstition that the sickness was caused by Apollo's arrows.

The Ecstasy of Saint Teresa, 1645–52
by Gianlorenzo Bernini (1598–1680)

Saint Teresa of Avila (1515–82) became a Carmelite nun at the age of
20 and devoted much of her life to reforming the order. She founded a
convent in Avila in 1562 and later introduced her nuns to houses in
Medina del Campo (1567), Toledo (1569), and Segovia (1574). In
addition to her work as a reformer, she also wrote a remarkable
biography, describing her spiritual development. Teresa's practical work,
however, made little impact on the arts. Instead, painters and sculptors
focused almost exclusively on the mystic visions that she experienced.

Bernini's celebrated sculpture portrays the most famous of these visions.
In this, Teresa was approached by an angel carrying a golden dart, which he
plunged into her heart. As the Holy Spirit pulsed into her body, Teresa fell
back, in a state of near collapse. Bernini's sculpture is a fairly literal
translation of the saint's account, but it is easy to see why the angel has been
compared to Eros, the god of love. His wielding of the arrow evokes obvious
memories of amorous, pagan legends, while the swooning expression of the
saint could easily be mistaken for physical, rather than spiritual ecstasy.

Saint Cecilia, 1897
by Gustave Moreau (1826–98)

In this mysterious, moonlit scene, Moreau presents a new slant on the legend
of Saint Cecilia. A group of angels approach the holy woman to warn her of
her impending martyrdom at the hands of the Roman authorities. According
to tradition, they tried initially to boil Cecilia alive in her own steam-room,
but she survived. After this, they decided to behead her, but the executioner
was unable to sever her head from her body – a detail that may explain why
the saint's hand strays nervously to her throat in Moreau's painting.

Moreau was one of the leading Symbolist painters and, in keeping with
their aims, he was more interested in conveying a dream-like mood than in
illustrating a precise narrative. Certainly he has taken a few liberties with
the legend. Cecilia's Roman house, for example, has been transformed into
some exotic, oriental palace.

Moreau produced several paintings of angels, often as part of some
highly idiosyncratic subjects. In *Dead Lyres* (*c.* 1897), he portrayed an
angel with a cross rising up from the remains of martyred poets.
On a more picturesque note, his *Angelic Traveller* (*c.* 1880) showed
an angel resting on the roof of Notre-Dame Cathedral, gazing down
wearily on the city below.

Saint Catherine, 1902
by Edward Reginald Frampton (1872–1923)

Frampton was a successful religious painter, who incorporated a wide variety
of influences into his versatile style. His father was a stained-glass designer,
which did much to influence his flat, decorative approach to composition.
He also drew considerable inspiration from Burne-Jones and the Symbolists.
He saw the former's retrospective exhibition at the New Gallery, following
Burne-Jones's death in 1898, and his pale, slender angels owe much to the
example of the Pre-Raphaelite artist. In addition, Frampton had close links
with the art scene in France. He exhibited at the Salon and painted a series
of pictures on Breton themes. In particular he tried to emulate the
'primitive' approach to religious painting, which Paul Gauguin
(1848–1903) and other members of the artists' colony in Brittany had
introduced in the late-nineteenth century. Frampton was also heavily
influenced by early Italian art. This may have persuaded him to try his
hand at mural painting. In the event, murals were to form a substantial part
of Frampton's output. He worked on a number of schemes in southern
England, at places such as Hastings, Ranmore and Southampton. He also
belonged to the Tempera Society and the Art Workers' Guild.

ANGELIC INTERPRETATIONS:

CLASSICAL TO ALLEGORICAL

ANGELIC INTERPRETATIONS:

CLASSICAL TO ALLEGORICAL

While the first part of this book showed images of angels taking part in specific events from sacred texts and the Christian tradition, this section looks at more liberal, playful and sometimes fanciful interpretations of what it means to be an angel. In some of the images the angels take part in apocryphal events and encounters, in others they are depicted solely as sacred musicians – stressing the importance of the role of music in the worship of God.

Angels are often referred to as guardians, and the concept of a spirit guide dates back to ancient times. Paintings depicting guardian angels, such as those shown on the following pages, can be comforting for children and parents alike, although the Christian Church has been inconsistent in acknowledging the existence of such beings. By contrast, the Muslim faith makes it clear that each child is assigned two guardian angels at birth. Also known as the honoured writers, one angel takes note of good deeds and other bad deeds. However, because of the prohibition of the depiction of natural forms in much of Islam, images of these angels are rare.

Some of the images in this part of the book examine the role of angels in legends, such as King Arthur and the Holy Grail. Others draw connections with the pagan gods and goddesses of antiquity. For example, what are the links between Cupid from classical mythology and Biblical cherubs? Is there a connection between angels on war memorials and the Nike or Goddess of Victory from Greek mythology? Such angels become allegorical figures, representing abstract concepts such as peace, love and death. In some interpretations of angels it can be difficult to draw a dividing line between them and fairies, creating the secular type of angel associated with magic and new age spirituality.

Guardian Angels

The idea of guardian angels has its origins in antiquity. The Assyrians and the Babylonians created sculptures of guardian figures, and the theory was supported by several classical philosophers. The Catholic authorities recognized and applauded the concept, but did not make it an article of faith. However, their defence of guardian angels was reaffirmed during the Counter Reformation, when the existence of all angels was called into question by Protestant leaders. The Papacy responded by encouraging the creation of a number of local feast days devoted to guardian angels. The first of these were granted to Cordoba (1579) and Valencia (1582).

During the Baroque period, an increasing number of altarpieces were dedicated to guardian angels. For artists, however, the emphasis on this subject gradually began to shift. Increasingly, painters highlighted the theme of the care and protection of children. In part, no doubt, this was caused by fears arising from the appalling rates of infant mortality, although some patrons may simply have remembered the famous passage from Saint Matthew's gospel: 'Except ye be converted, and become as little children, ye shall not enter into the kingdom of heaven...Take heed that ye despise not one of these little ones; for I say unto you, That in heaven their angels do always behold the face of my Father.' (Matthew 18:3 and 10).

The Guardian Angel, 1656
by Pietro da Cortona
(1596–1669)

The concept of the guardian angel is not specifically laid down in the Scriptures, but it was welcomed and accepted by many early theologians. Saint Jerome (342–420), for example, wrote in one of his Commentaries: 'How great the dignity of the soul, since each one has from his birth an angel commissioned to guard it'. This link with the soul had appeared in paintings by the Middle Ages, when angels were often shown carrying away the soul – represented by a tiny human figure – after a person had died. This was most common in scenes of martyrdom or the Crucifixion (*see* page 103).

The subject developed further at the time of the Counter Reformation. At this stage, the angel was frequently portrayed as an adult, leading a child or young adult by the hand. Often, the scenes were based on pictures of *Tobias and the Angel*, emphasizing the protection that a guardian angel could provide, during the dangerous business of travelling. However, the older idea of an angel preserving the soul after death also remained in currency. This is probably the meaning behind Pietro's picture. The angel starts to rise off the ground and points towards heaven, indicating to the child that this is where they are going.

The Light of the World, date unknown
by Frederic James Shields
(1833–1911)

Shields' devotional picture is about the salvation of humanity. The Christ Child walks along a narrow path, bringing light and hope into the darkness. The image of the lantern comes from the Bible ('Thy word is a lamp unto my feet, and a light unto my path', Psalm 119:105), as is the metaphor about light ('I am the light of the world: he that followeth me shall not walk in darkness, but shall have the light of life, John 8:12). The child's face is steadfast and serious, aware of the sacrifice that is to come. Under his foot he crushes the snake, symbolizing the vanquishing of sin.

The artist drew his inspiration from Holman Hunt's picture of the same name. This featured the adult Christ alone, without the angel, but the basic message was the same. Hunt's painting had received a mixed reception when it was first exhibited in 1854, but by the end of the century it had become an institution. It was so famous that it was sent on a tour of the colonies from 1905–07. Shields was a follower of the Pre-Raphaelites and was personally acquainted with Hunt. He was also extremely devout. Every day he began his journal with the words: 'wash, prayer, Bible, breakfast'.

FOUR CORNERS TO MY BED, DATE UNKNOWN
by Isobel Lilian Gloag (1868–1917)

Gloag's painting is a wonderfully literal depiction of an old nursery rhyme or prayer:

> *Matthew, Mark, Luke and John,*
> *Bless the bed that I lie on!*
> *Four corners to my bed,*
> *Four angels round my head:*
> *One to watch, one to pray,*
> *And two to bear my soul away!*

The verse dates back at least as far as the mid-seventeenth century, when it was included in a book called *A Candle in the Dark* (1656). It remained popular in the Victorian era, however, when the threat of infant mortality loomed over every parent. Gloag has conceived her angels as young girls wearing voluminous robes and playing medieval instruments. Three of them are virtually identical, while the fourth kneels by the cot and prays. Her hair and clothing set her apart from the musical trio. Perhaps she is a departed member of the family, praying for a younger sibling. Gloag's parents were Scottish, but she was trained in London and Paris and exhibited regularly at the Royal Academy. Her taste for rich, medieval settings harks back to the Pre-Raphaelites, while her sensuous depictions of femmes fatales link her with the Symbolist movement.

L'ANGE GARDIEN ('THE GUARDIAN ANGEL'), c. 1898
by Gabriel-Joseph-Marie-Augustin Ferrier (1847–1914)

The concept of the guardian angel was derived from a few biblical references. In the Gospel of Saint Matthew, Christ mentions how the 'little ones' have 'their angels [who] do always behold the face' of God (Matthew 18:10). There is also a specific example in the Book of Tobit, in the Apocrypha, where Raphael acts as the guardian angel of Tobias. The idea was taken up by the Catholic Church: several popes introduced specific feast days for 'our guardian angels', and in a number of Baroque churches there are special chapels dedicated to them.

In artistic terms the subject evolved from early depictions of death scenes. These would often portray the soul as a naked infant being lifted out of the body and carried up to heaven by a small angel. These images strengthened the association between children and guardian angels, although in purely doctrinal terms the Church made it clear that adults also had their spiritual protectors. Nevertheless, nineteenth-century depictions of the subject were usually focused on infants, in part no doubt because of the health risks that they faced. Ferrier is mainly remembered now as a teacher rather than for his own work. His best-known pupil was the Cubist artist Fernand Léger.

THE ANGEL OF MONS c. 1914
by an unknown artist

Not all angelic visions are confined to altarpieces and saints' biographies. During the First World War, there was a popular belief that a group of beleaguered British soldiers had been rescued by the intervention of an angelic force. This saviour, who became known as 'the Angel of Mons', was pictured on ephemera of all kinds, including posters, postcards and newspaper illustrations. This particular image comes from the cover of some sheet music – a waltz composed in honour of the angel.

The story revolved around the Battle of Mons, which took place in August 1914. Heavily outnumbered, the British Expeditionary Force was forced to retreat from this, but reports began to circulate about a supernatural force that came to their aid. At first, the nature of this force seemed very confused. Some viewed it as an angel of the Lord, riding a white horse and wielding a flaming sword; others, however, talked of phantom bowmen, apparently resurrected from the time of Agincourt. By 1915, the rumours were sufficiently widespread to prompt a study by the Society for Psychical Research. They found no evidence of any miraculous event, but the authorities made little attempt to suppress the story, realizing that it was helping to boost morale.

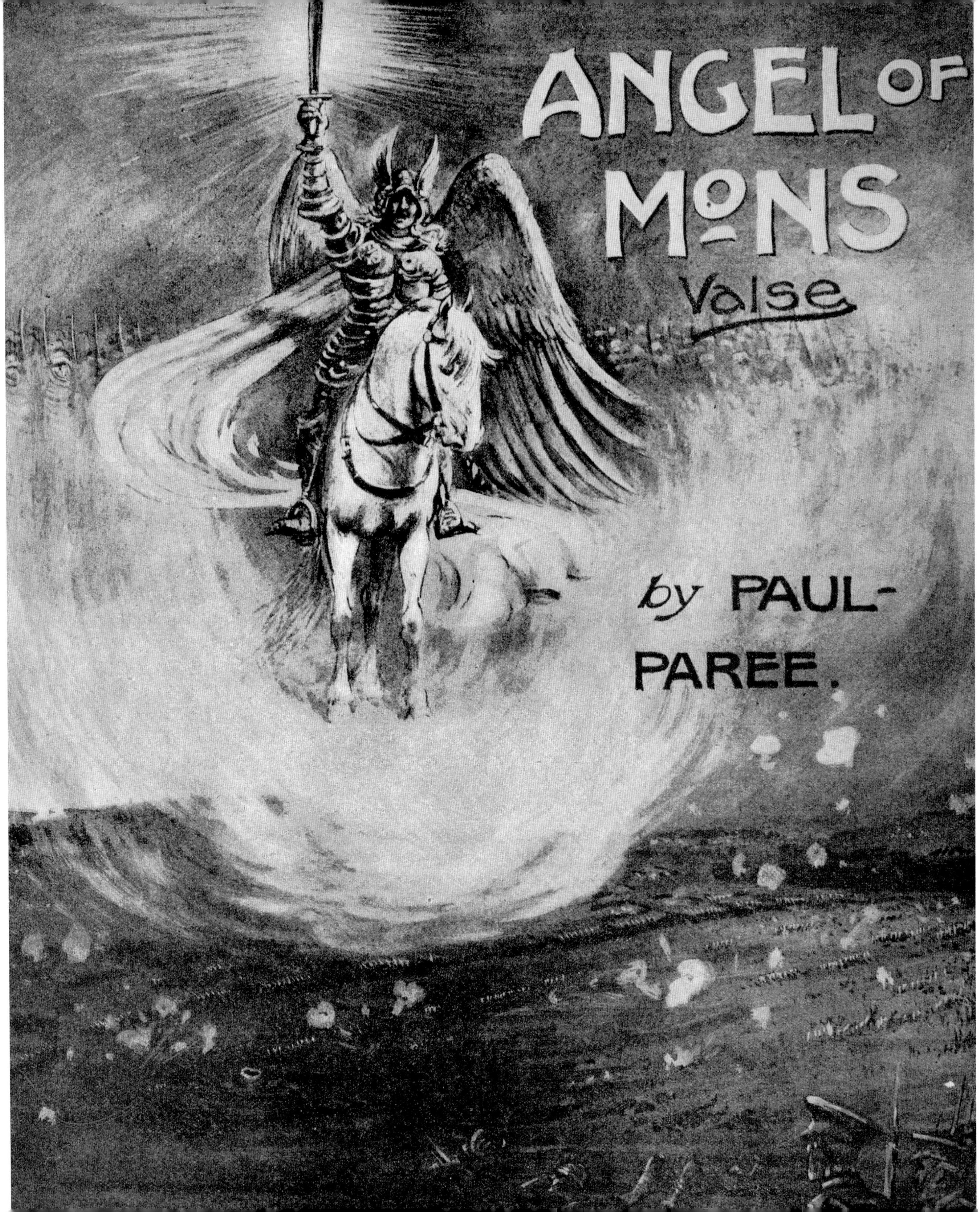
ANGEL OF MONS
Valse
by PAUL-PAREE.

Victorian Angels

The revival of interest in angels, which occurred during the Victorian era, was spearheaded by the Pre-Raphaelites. Founded in 1848 by Dante Gabriel Rossetti and others, the group shared a love of all things medieval. In particular, they were passionate about early Italian art prior to the time of Raphael (1483–1520) and tried to recapture the simplicity of its approach.

At the same time, they were also fascinated by Arthurian legends and it is no accident that their earliest joint project was the creation of a series of murals at the Oxford Union, illustrating scenes from Malory's *Morte d'Arthur*. Other artists followed suit, but there was an increasing emphasis on the religious undercurrents of the tales. Gradually, the Quest for the Holy Grail became the most popular theme.

Later in the century, a second generation of Pre-Raphaelite artists gathered around Edward Burne-Jones and William Morris. The latter founded a highly influential manufacturing and decorating firm, which benefited greatly from the High Church revival taking place at the time. As a result, they received numerous commissions to redecorate churches. In terms of angels, their stained-glass windows were particularly important. Burne-Jones' graceful, androgynous figures provided a lead that many other artists were to follow.

Sir Galahad, 1891
by Robert Burns
(1869–1941)

Sir Galahad was 'the spotless knight', the purest and most noble of King Arthur's followers. The son of Lancelot and Elaine, he was the last to take his seat at the Round Table, the seat known as the 'siege perilous', which was reserved for the greatest knight of all. Galahad merited this title not just because of his strength and valour, but also because of his flawless character. This enabled him to succeed in the quest for the Holy Grail. Here, three angels appear to the knight in a vision, together with the Grail itself – the chalice used by Christ at the Last Supper.

Arthurian subjects became extremely popular during the Victorian period. In part this stemmed from various artistic influences: the novels of Sir Walter Scott (1771–1832), the poems of Alfred, Lord Tennyson (1809–92), and the paintings of the Pre-Raphaelites. On another level, though, it echoed a revival of interest in the concept of chivalry. For many Victorians, Sir Galahad's blend of courage, honour and piety made him the ideal role model for the modern gentleman. As a result, knightly images were featured on a wide variety of objects, ranging from sporting trophies (such as the Queen's Cup, Ascot) to war memorials and school certificates.

Lancelot's Vision of the Holy Grail, 1893
by Frederick Hamilton Jackson
(1848–1923)

According to some accounts, the Holy Grail made its first appearance at Arthur's court at Pentecost. While the knights were dining, there was a roll of thunder, followed by a burst of radiant light. Then the Grail appeared in the great hall, covered by a samite veil. The light was so dazzling that nobody could see who was holding it, as it floated around the chamber. In its wake, it left a fragrance so sweet and overpowering that the men could not move or speak.

After the Grail had gone, the knights recovered their senses and talked amongst themselves about seeing it again. Their greatest desire, though, was to see the Grail in all its glory, not hidden under a veil. This had not been possible, they decided, because their vision had been impaired by their sins. Only when they were in a state of perfect grace, would they be able to see this spiritual treasure.

Lancelot joined the quest to find the Grail but, like most of his fellow knights, he failed in his search. The nearest he came to it was at a ruined chapel in a forest. Through an iron grille, he could see the Grail, still veiled, upon the altar, but his sins prevented him from entering.

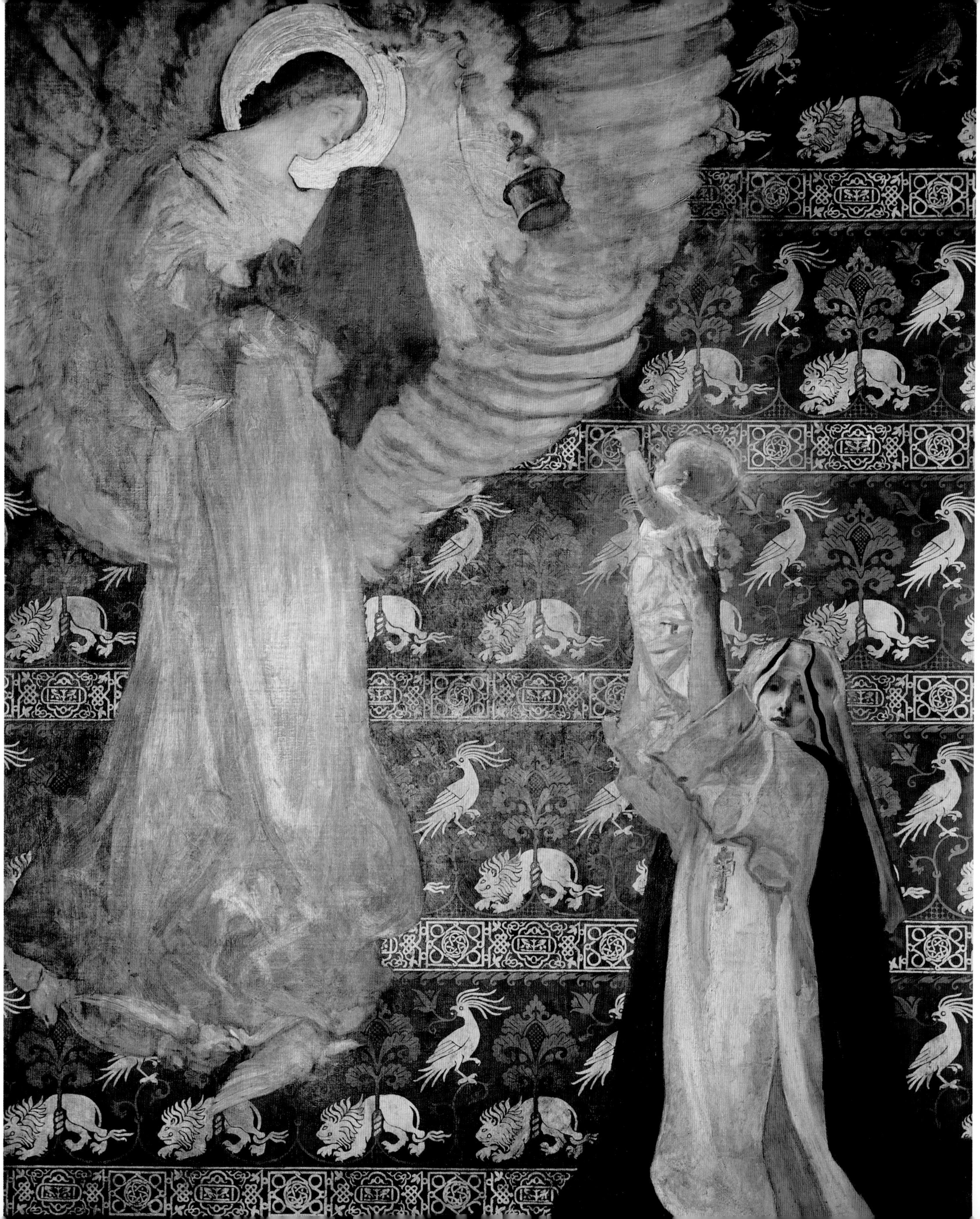

Galahad visited by an Angel, 1895
by Edwin Austin Abbey (1852–1911)

At the height of his career, Edwin Abbey (1852–1911) was commissioned to produce a major decorative scheme for the Book Delivery Room at the new Boston Public Library. He chose as his theme an ambitious Arthurian scheme, *The Quest and Achievement of the Holy Grail*. The project consisted of fifteen separate panels, created in a sumptuous mix of oils and gold leaf.

This is the first picture in the series. It depicts an episode during the childhood of Sir Galahad, when he was being raised by nuns. On this occasion, he is experiencing a mystic vision, in which he sees an angel carrying the Holy Grail, concealed under a veil. Alongside her there is a dove bearing a golden censer (incense burner). The vision is so dazzling that the nun cannot look on it, but Galahad has no such problems and reaches out a hand, towards the Grail.

As in many of the other Grail paintings from this period, there is an obvious mingling of Christian and Arthurian material. The ultimate success of Galahad's quest, for example, was partly attributed to the legend that he was a distant descendant of Joseph of Arimathaea, the Biblical figure who gave Christ his own tomb.

Mors Janua Vitae, 1866
by Sir Joseph Noël Paton (1821–1901)

Away from his fairy paintings, Paton also produced a series of sombre, religious pictures. When he first exhibited *Mors Janua Vitae* ('*Death is the Gateway to [everlasting] Life*'), he included a lengthy extract from *The Good Fight* by A. Graves, which explained the allegory in detail. A Christian soldier is mortally wounded. Weary and in pain he follows a shadowy figure, who leads him through a dark and barren landscape to the gates of death. There he is rewarded for his faithful service: 'And the Shadow spake, and its voice was as the voice of an angel: "Thou hast been faithful unto death; the Lord will give thee a crown of Life." Then was the veil of the Darkness rent asunder and lo! the Shadow was clothed with light, as with a garment of rejoicing…'.

This type of approach was not unusual for the funerary art of the period. Both Harry Bates (1850–1914) and Sir Alfred Gilbert (1854–1934) produced sculptures entitled *Mors Janua Vitae* and there was a fashion for tomb effigies, which portrayed the deceased in the guise of a knight. The most celebrated was Edward Henry Corbourld's memorial portrait of Prince Albert (1819–61), which showed the subject in full armour and included the inscription, 'I have fought a good fight; I have finished the struggle; therefore the crown of the righteous is awaiting me'.

HOW AN ANGEL ROWED SIR GALAHAD ACROSS THE DERN MERE, 1888
by Sir Joseph Noël Paton (1821–1901)

Paton painted at least three pictures on the subject of Sir Galahad, the others being *Sir Galahad and his Angel* and *Sir Galahad's Vision of the Sangreal*. The theme had a particularly strong appeal for him, as it combined his passionate interest in romantic medievalism with his personal commitment to the Christian faith. Paton's fascination with the Middle Ages came partly from his father, who had worked as a fabric designer but became engrossed in antiquarian matters, and partly from the novels of Sir

Walter Scott (1771–1832). The most tangible evidence of this fascination could be found at Paton's home, where he amassed a most remarkable collection of arms and armour. He had inherited a few pieces from his father, but as soon as his career took off he began buying in earnest. The collection was so impressive that it was eventually acquired by the National Museum of Scotland. Inevitably Paton was keen to introduce aspects of his hobby into his work. In addition to his Arthurian subjects, armour appears in a number of religious, allegorical and genre pictures. In *The Choice* an armoured knight is torn between the attractions of an angel and a seductive sorceress, while *I Wonder Who Lived in There* is a charming depiction of the artist's son, staring into an empty helmet.

The Vision at the Martyr's Well, date UNKNOWN
by George Henry Boughton (1833–1905)

Many Victorians had an ambivalent attitude towards religion. Most were deeply pious even though they were capable of approaching sacred manifestations with a spirit of scientific enquiry, rather than through faith alone. In the 1880s, for example, there was considerable controversy after several people experienced a vision similar to this arguably angelic one at Llanthony Priory in Wales. The witnesses saw 'a most Majestic Heavenly Form, robed in flowing drapery', which they assumed was 'Our Ladye'. Some were prepared to take the miracle on trust, yet this was also the period when the Society for Psychical Research was founded (1882). This influential body, which was to include William Gladstone (1809–98), Alfred, Lord Tennyson (1809–92) and Lewis Carroll (1832–98) among its membership, made a particular study of spirit photography, where ghostly images similar to this vision were captured on film.

Boughton has a curious claim to fame, as a man who inspired Vincent Van Gogh (1853–90). At the start of his career the Dutchman lived for a time in London, where he worked as a teacher and also acted as a lay preacher in his spare time. In this capacity he preached a sermon at Richmond, which was inspired directly by one of Boughton's canvases, *God Speed!* (1874).

Adolescentiae Somnia Celestiae (detail), date unknown
by John Staines Babb (fl. 1870–1900)

Pictures of dreams and sleeping were very fashionable in the nineteenth century. Modern critics have questioned whether some of these pictures may have been influenced by the effect of drugs, and Fitzgerald's dream pictures, in particular, have come under scrutiny – one could argue that the angels here may be allegorical representations of sleep-inducing drugs.

Opiates were both legal and readily available at the time. Indeed, Britain had entered into two Opium Wars (1839–42 and 1856–60) with China in order to maintain this trade. In addition, Thomas De Quincey's (1785–1859) *Confessions of an English Opium Eater* was greeted with praise rather than recrimination when it was published in 1821–22. Nevertheless reservations were voiced later in the century, when the addictive properties of opium and laudanum became more evident. The Pharmacy Act of 1868 began the process of restricting their sale, and in the 1880s a series of cautionary books were published. Most notable of these was H.H. Kane's *Drugs that Enslave: the Opium, Morphine, Chloral and Hash Habits* (1881).

Dante's Dream at the Time of the Death of Beatrice, c. 1900
by A.C. Lalli, after Dante Gabriel Rossetti
(Rossetti 1828–1882)

The composition of this painting is based on part of the *Vita Nuova* by Dante Aligheri (1265–1321):

> Then Love said, 'Now shall all things be made clear:
> Come and behold our lady where she lies.'
> These 'wildering phantasies
> Then carried me to see my lady dead.
> Even as I there was led,
> Her ladies with a veil were covering her;
> And with her was such very humbleness
> That she appeared to say, 'I am at peace.'

Rossetti painted several versions of the subject, culminating in a huge canvas in 1871, the largest picture he ever produced. The red birds are messengers of death, while the angelic figure of Love, also in red, leads the poet to the deathbed of his beloved. The floor is strewn with red poppies, which symbolize dreams.

Rossetti had close links with the poet. His father was a renowned Dante scholar and named his son after the writer. The artist shared his father's passion for Dante and painted numerous pictures based on his verses. Through him, Dante's work also proved a fruitful source of inspiration for other members of the Pre-Raphaelite circle.

The Music of Angels

From the early Middle Ages onwards, artists associated angels with music-making. They were shown carrying out this activity in almost every imaginable situation. There were angels performing celestial concerts in the Court of Heaven, as they congregated around the thrones of the Almighty or the Virgin; there were angels playing music when they appeared to the shepherds, at the Nativity of Christ; they were performing as the saved were led into Paradise, at the time of the Last Judgement; and they were the eternal attendants of Mary, whether in devotional paintings of the Virgin and Child, or during her Assumption into heaven.

There were numerous passages in the Bible to promote this link. The descriptions of heaven in the Book of Revelations, for example, mentioned music ('And I heard a voice from heaven...and I heard the voice of harpers harping with their harps; And they sung as it were a new song before the throne.' Rev. 14:2–3). In addition, the traditional division of angels into nine choirs (*see* Introduction) became linked with the concept of the universal harmony, generated by the music of the spheres. The idea was also popularized by accounts of visions. One famous example, by a monk of Eynsham, emphasized the sublime nature of the music of Paradise, which sounded as if every bell in the world was pealing.

Angels making Music, completed 1432
by Jan and Hubert van Eyck (c. 1390–1441)

This opulent panel is part of Van Eyck's most imposing masterpiece, *The Ghent Altarpiece*. When it was opened up, this remarkable artwork displayed 12 separate scenes, on two tiers. This picture is situated in the upper level, to the right of a portrait of John the Baptist, and forms a pair with *Angels Singing*, on the left-hand side. Its location, close to the depictions of God and the Virgin, probably explains why these angels are far more richly attired than their counterparts in *The Adoration of the Lamb* (*see* page 79) in the lower tier. The two scenes are linked, however, by the emblem of the Mystic Lamb, which can be seen in the decoration on the floor, along with Christ's monogram and various other religious symbols.

There is another, even more striking difference between the musical angels and those featured elsewhere on the altarpiece – they have no wings. The reason for this was sheer practicality. It would have been hard to combine the wings elegantly with the heavy, brocade vestments, and even more difficult to squeeze them into the cramped picture space. Whilst this might be regarded as a simple act of artistic licence, it also demonstrates that, even in religious circles, there was no clear consensus about the appearance of angels.

Angel and Guitar, 1499–1502
by Luca Signorelli (1441–1523)

Angel and Guitar is a detail from *Fall of the Rebel Angels* by Luca Signorelli. The fresco painting is to be found in Orvieto Cathedral. In 1447 the artist Fra Angelico, the Dominican friar, began the fresco scenes of the *Last Judgement* in the cathedral. This work was later continued by Luca Signorelli. His series of semicircular portrayals of life, death, damnation and resurrection complement the earlier work. Most of the scenes depict the harsh brutality of death and damnation but Signorelli is able to portray the sweeter side of life and resurrection in the portrayal of this angel.

The image depicts a beautiful angel with a head of long golden ringlets. The angel is open-mouthed, singing sweetly whilst accompanying himself on a stringed musical instrument, which would be recognized today as a guitar. Large pale blue wings are outstretched behind his body, which is clothed in a simple garment with many folds. Signorelli's depiction of the angel is quite different to Fra Angelico's. Here the angel is a young person who could be recognized in the streets of Orvieto, rather than Fra Angelico's depiction of angels in the Gothic manner as reserved, ethereal messengers of God.

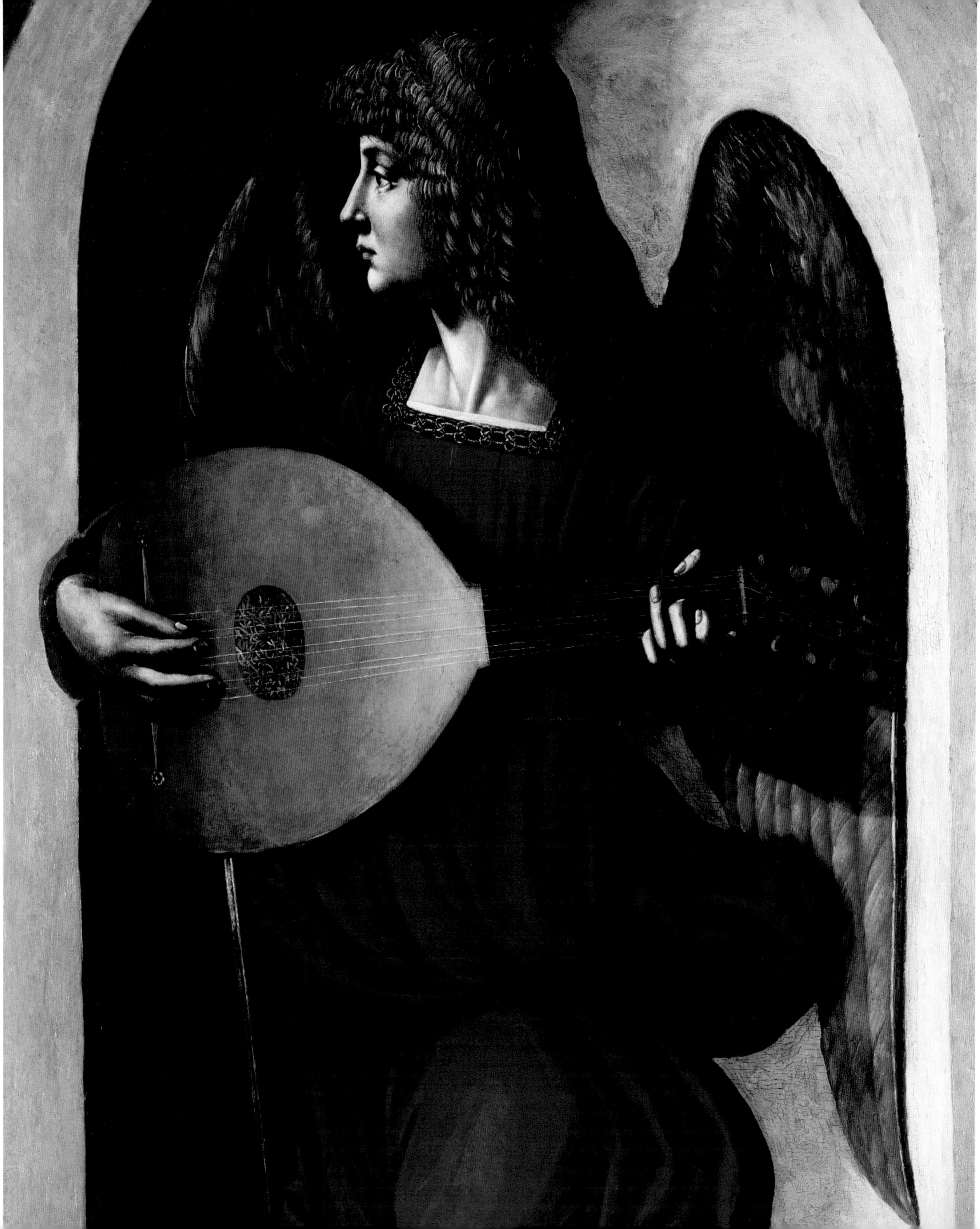

An Angel in Red with a Lute, c. 1490–99
by the De Predis brothers (da Vinci's assistants)
(c. 1455–after 1508)

This angel formed a side panel on one of Leonardo da Vinci's (1452–1519) most celebrated paintings, the *Virgin of the Rocks*. Leonardo produced two versions of this subject, one of which is now in the National Gallery, London, while the other is in the Louvre. The original commission came from the Confraternity of the Immaculate Conception in Milan, who wanted an altarpiece for their chapel in the church of San Francesco il Grande. The first contract was signed in 1480, but there was a second agreement in 1483 and the commission eventually became a long, protracted affair. Leonard worked on the project intermittently between *c*. 1491 and 1508.

The complexity of this arrangement gives some idea of the way that angels were used in altarpieces. The panels of the Virgin and the musical angels (*see* also this page) formed a small but essential part of a huge, wooden altarpiece, which also featured a profusion of carvings. It was the artist's job to colour and gild the statues, and to provide painted panels for the remaining sections – in this case, the Virgin of the Rocks in the centre and side-panels showing 'four angels playing instruments and singing'. Unfortunately the original altarpiece has not survived, so it is unclear if more angels were produced for his commission.

An Angel in Green with a Vielle, c. 1490–99
by the De Predis brothers (da Vinci's assistants)
(c. 1455–after 1508)

Together with *An Angel in Red with a Lute* (*see* opposite), this formed part of one Leonardo da Vinci's (1452–1519) most famous altarpieces, the *Virgin of the Rocks*. This was a substantial commission so, in keeping with normal practice, he employed assistants. In this case they were the half-brothers, Ambrogio and Evangelista de Predis, who both came from Milan. Leonardo painted the central panel, while they produced the side-panels, under his supervision. The precise division of labour between the brothers is unclear. This illustrates the role that pictures of angels played in many altarpieces. They were decorative, subsidiary elements that could complement any religious scene, but were rarely essential.

This painting is of particular interest to musicologists because of its detailed depiction of an obsolete instrument. The vielle was developed during the Middle Ages, when it became particularly popular with the troubadours. It was a bowed instrument, similar in many ways to a fiddle, although its shape is slightly different. It was highly versatile and was widely used in both secular and sacred music. The name survives in the *vielle à roue*, the French term for a hurdy-gurdy, which is played with a wheel rather than a bow.

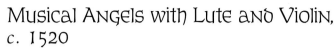

Musical Angels with Lute and Violin, c. 1520
by Lattanzio di Niccolò di Liberatore da Folignos
(fl. 1480–1527)

This painting, one of a pair, (*see* pages 142–43), depicts two naked infant angels with wings outstretched. They sit amidst clouds in the celestial sky. The angels are in concert and each earnestly plays his stringed wooden instrument: one the lute, the other the violin. The tiny fingers of the lute player pluck at the strings; the violinist holds the instrument wedged in to his shoulder, the bow stretched across the bridge of the violin. They are in deep concentration as they play; the cheeks of their faces are rosy with the effort of playing. The lute instrument with its bulging, pear shaped body, and the smaller violin were recognized and used in paintings as symbols of Music personified, one of the seven Liberal Arts. Concerts of angels were often used to narrate stories of love; the angels sitting above, or surrounding, the main subject.

Italian artist Lattanzio di Niccolò, was born in Foligno, close to Perugia, in Umbria. He was the son of the painter Niccolò da Foligno (1430–1502) – both are less well-known artists of the Renaissance. They worked together on many commissions, including the high altarpiece of San Francesco in Cannara (1482).

Musical Angels with Zither and Horn, c. 1520
by Lattanzio di Niccoli di Liberatore da Foligno (fl. 1480–1527)

This painting, one of a pair, depicts two infant angels, naked but for their colourful wings, which are outstretched. They sit amidst fluffy clouds. The angels are in concert and each plays a wooden instrument: one the zither (a flat sound box with numerous strings), the other a horn. The horn player looks toward the spectator; the zither player looks down at the instrument, concentrating on the strings he is plucking and the melody he is creating. Paired with *Musical Angels with Lute and Violin* the four would be depicted together in concert. Their instruments are attributes and signifiers of Music, one of the seven Liberal Arts.

Angels, especially infants, are often depicted as adorable chubby children. Here however, they are less so – the use of harsh colours and the heavy thighs and calves of the angels lead one to suggest that this is a painting in the Mannerist style, which became popular toward the end of the High Renaissance, when artists moved away from idealized portrayals, and exaggerated the human form.

Italian artist Lattanzio di Niccolò was born in Foglino, close to Perugia, in Umbria. He was the son of the painter Niccolò da Foligno. Father and son often worked together on commissions, usually for religious works of art.

Musical Angel, 1522
by Rosso Fiorentino (1494–1540)

If Walt Disney had decided to make a picture of a cherub, it might well have turned out like this. In an amusing variant on the theme of angel musicians, a tiny, curly-haired cherub struggles to play a lute that is far too big for him. Other painters tried to mimic this idea, but no one managed to execute it with quite the same charm as Rosso.

In common with some of his fellow artists Rosso developed more than one way of portraying angels. When he included cherubic infants in his pictures they were usually employed in a decorative or humorous manner. In his *Madonna with Saints*, for instance, there are two tiny angels in the foreground who chatter away in a childish manner and completely ignore the holy figures that surround them. In his *Dead Christ Supported by Angels*, though, there is no such levity. The angels are young men, rather than children, and their sombre expressions mirror the gravity of the theme.

This type of versatility was Rosso's trademark. He was an independent, strong-willed character, who refused to accept the authority of any master and had a mischievous sense of humour. According to an early biographer he used to torment the local monks by letting his pet monkey loose on them.

Saint Cecilia playing the Spinet with an Angel, c. 1620
by Orazio Gentileschi (1563–1639)

Saint Cecilia was an early saint and martyr who is believed to have lived in the late second or early third century. There are many colourful legends about her life but few genuine facts are known. In Western art she appeared principally as the patron saint of music, and was usually portrayed with a portative (portable) organ. However, this instrument had become obsolete by the sixteenth century, so some painters replaced it with a newer model. The spinet, for example, would have seemed a very modern instrument at this time. Cecilia's playing style often looks very odd because artists were anxious to stress that she had no interest in earthly music, listening only to the heavenly concert that she heard in her head. As a result she was often shown playing with her eyes closed or looking

away from her instrument. Here, for example, she studiously ignores the sheet of music that is held up for her.

There was renewed interest in the saint in the seventeenth century. This followed the rediscovery of her relics in 1599, during the course of restoration work at her church in Rome (St Cecilia in Trastevere). This led a number of artists to paint scenes from her life, among them both Orazio Gentileschi (1563–1639) and his daughter Artemisia (1593–1652/53).

O Salutaris Hostia, date unknown
by George Wooliscroft Rhead (1855–1920)

O saving victim opening wide / The gates of heaven to all below,
Our foes press on from every side; / Thy help supply, thy strength bestow.

Rhead's picture takes its name from a Latin hymn – 'O Salutaris Hostia' ('O Saving Victim') is the first line from the penultimate stanza of 'Verbum Supernum Prodiens', composed by Saint Thomas Aquinas (c. 1225–74):

The hymn was originally used for the celebration of Mass at Lauds, during the Feast of Corpus Christi. Aquinas was asked to produce the verses by Pope Urban IV (1261–64), when he introduced the feast in 1264. Since

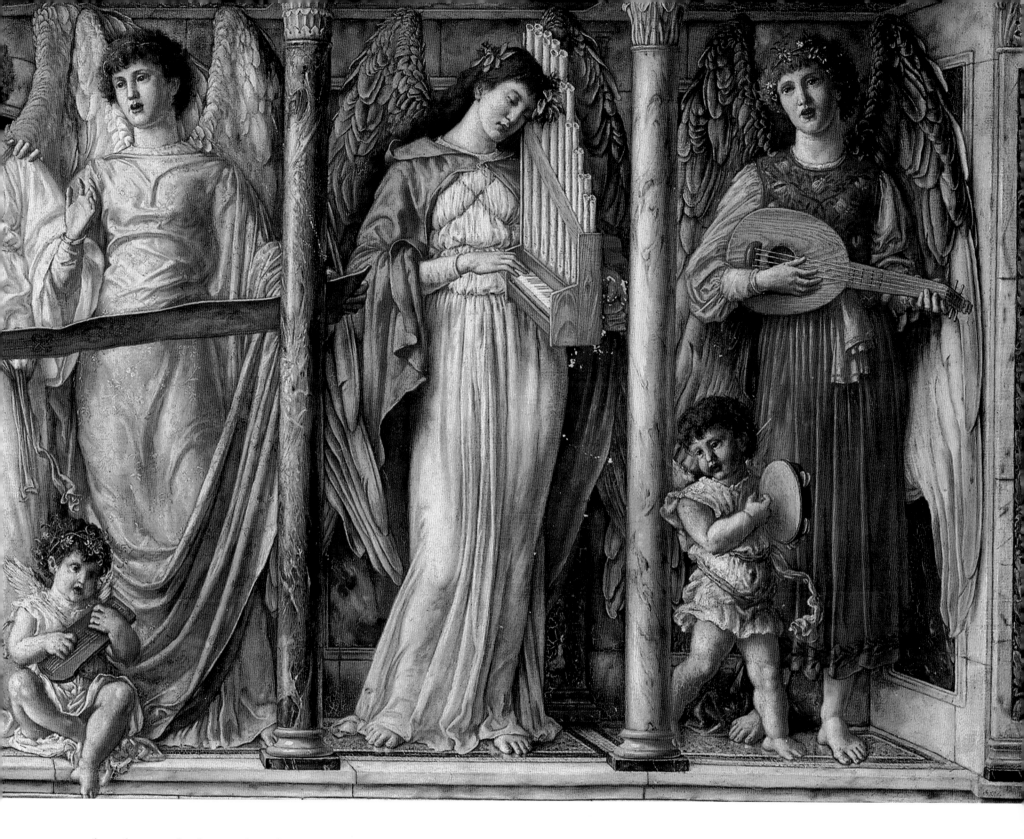

then, the prayer has been used in other services, principally for the benediction of the blessed sacrament.

George Rhead was a versatile artist and teacher who produced etchings and ceramics, but was best known for his book illustrations. He often collaborated with his brother Louis (1858–1926), most notably on the illustrations for Tennyson's Idylls of the King (1859).

In this painting his angelic orchestra is depicted in a Pre-Raphaelite manner, mimicking the style of early Italian art. Rhead deliberately attempted to create an archaic effect, depicting antique instruments, even though in his original Italian models these items would have been contemporary.

H. PINTA

L'Ange Musicien ('Musician Angel'), 1892
by Henri Ludovic Marius Pinta (1856–unknown)

Since the Middle Ages, celestial choirs and orchestras have been an ever-present feature of Christian art. Their popularity stems from the exhortation in the Book of Psalms that the faithful should make use of music in paying homage to God:

> *Praise ye the Lord… / Praise him with trumpet's sound;*
> *His praise with psaltery advance;*
> *With timbrel, harp, string'd instruments, and organs, in the dance.*
> *Praise him on cymbals loud: Him praise on cymbals sounding high.*
> *Let each breathing thing praise the Lord…* (Psalm 150)

Many nineteenth-century artists took these words literally and deliberately portrayed their angelic musicians with a range of archaic instruments.

Henri Pinta was a French history painter and muralist, who produced much of his best work in the Marseille area. His most celebrated pictures are probably the murals that he produced for the church of Notre Dame du Mont.

Titania's Awakening, 1896
by Charles Sims (1873–1928)

When Queen Titania awoke, the spell was broken and she saw Bottom in his true colours. Then Oberon called for soft, magical music, which allowed the fairies to dance while the mortals remained asleep. The title inevitably conjures up this scene, but the painting itself was produced during Sims' Symbolist period, when the artist was more interested in evoking a poetic mood than any narrative event. The otherworldly musician wears the thick plumage of an angel, not the gossamer wings of a fairy. There are no celebrations here. The tone is elegiac and autumnal, as though her ethereal music is plucking the leaves from the trees.

Sims trained in Paris at the Académie Julian, but spent most of his career in England. His outstanding technique won him great critical acclaim, particularly at the Royal Academy where his breezy, outdoor subjects were especially popular. The latter part of his career, however, was clouded by tragedy. His son was killed in the trenches and he himself was traumatized by his experiences as a war artist. The strange, semi-abstract Spirituals, which Sims painted after the war, offered evidence of his emotional turmoil. He eventually took his own life in 1928.

An Angel Piping to the Souls in Hell, *c.* 1916
by Evelyn de Morgan (1850–1919)

This scene is reminiscent of some nineteenth-century depictions of Dante's Inferno, a source that was popular with some of the Pre-Raphaelites. Nevertheless, the picture was chiefly a response to the horrors of the First World War. De Morgan was appalled by the carnage in the trenches and did her best to raise money to alleviate the suffering. This culminated in the Red Cross Benefit Exhibition, which she helped to stage in 1916. De Morgan contributed 13 pictures to the show, including this one. In her will she also gave instructions for some of her paintings to be sold off, to raise funds for St Dunstan's, a charity for blind soldiers.

At this stage of her career de Morgan was producing complex allegorical pictures, very much in the manner of G.F. Watts (1817–1904). In this instance, the entry in the exhibition catalogue gave a clue to the picture's meaning: 'Come from afar, the Angel bends over the abyss and pipes her angelic strains, that the flame-tossed souls in Hell may hear the distant music'. In essence she was hoping that, like the angel, she and the charities she supported could bring some crumbs of comfort to the soldiers, who were going through their own personal hell.

Cherubim to Cherubs

In the traditional division of angels, cherubim were classed alongside seraphim and thrones as the most exalted rank of celestial beings. These three were closest to God, devoting their time to perpetual worship. They were also described by David as the 'chariot of God', because they transported him on their wings.

In the Old Testament, cherubim were frequently mentioned in an artistic context. Jewish craftsmen made carvings of them for the Mercy Seat on the lid of the Ark. Images of them were also embroidered on the Veil of the Tabernacle, and engraved on the panelling in the Temple of Jerusalem.

In Western art their depiction varied considerably. When they were shown in the Court of Heaven, they were often portrayed simply as a child's head, surrounded by six wings. They were normally coloured blue and could be pictured with a book. When they were shown in connection with earthly events, however, they were usually given human form. The cherubim standing guard at the gate of Eden, following the expulsion of Adam and Eve, is a typical example. By the Renaissance the origins of this type of angel were increasingly ignored. Instead they became indistinguishable from the cupids that had evolved from classical art and cherubim became 'cherubs' – a word that can mean simply a sweet and innocent child.

The Sistine Madonna (detail), c. 1513
by Raphael (1483–1520)

The depiction of tiny angels could create problems for some artists. On the one hand, there was a temptation to portray them like normal infants, with a natural sense of wonder and incomprehension at the miraculous events happening around them. On the other hand, angels were not children; they knew and understood the sacred significance of their situation. No artist managed to maintain this delicate balance more astutely than Raphael.

These two angels can be found at the foot of Raphael's most celebrated painting of Mary, his *Sistine Madonna*. In this, the Virgin and Child float serenely on a cloud, accompanied by Saint Sixtus and Saint Barbara. The angels have the faces of children, but they look up reflectively at this glimpse of heaven.

Ostensibly the subject of this picture was chosen because the painting was destined for the church of San Sisto (Saint Sixtus) in Piacenza. However, the saint bears the features of Raphael's most important patron, Pope Julius II – the man who commissioned *The Liberation of Saint Peter* (*see* page 111). Julius died in 1513 and there are suggestions that this picture was designed as a memorial to him. It is said to have been carried in his funeral procession.

Cherubs in the Clouds, date unknown
Charles Augustus Henry Lutyens (1829–1915)

This painting by Charles Lutyens is a Victorian poesy of prettiness. The dimpled cherubs with chubby cheeks and legs hold on to each other whilst they look through the clouds toward Earth. Lutyens, recognized for his romanticized depictions, creates a vision of heavenly happiness. Each cherub has wings, which are just visible. The cherub angel to the left looks to the other to speak. He holds on to her, perhaps to steady himself in the fluffy, windy cloud formations. He holds a posy of colourful flowers in his hand, perhaps a symbol of love. The other cherub looks away, trying to cover her head with a celestial cloth. Flowers fall between the two cherubs. This could be a personification of young love, in its first throes. Each angel is unsure of the next stage of courtship.

Captain Charles Lutyens left the army to become a successful painter, who exhibited at the Royal Academy, London. He and his wife had a family of ten children, one of which was the globally famous architect Edward Lutyens.

The Sleeping Angel, 1897
by Léon Jean Basile Perrault (1832–1908)

Perrault found a ready market for his sentimental paintings of chubby infants. The Victorians and their French counterparts adored pictures of children, whether playing, in the home or in images of bereavement as here. Throughout the century the subject of childbirth produced mixed emotions. There was joy of course, but also fear. The procedure could be lethal, both for the mother and the child. In 1901, for example, the official statistic for deaths in childbirth was 4,400 in England and Wales, which was almost certainly an underestimate of the real figure. For mothers the average mortality rate was an appalling 4.8 per thousand live births. This rate did not actually drop below one per thousand until as late as 1944. And even if the difficulties of childbirth were successfully negotiated, the first few years of life remained perilous. In 1899 the mortality rate for infants under the age of one was 163 per thousand. The problems stemmed from a number of factors, most notably poor living conditions, the absence of organized antenatal care and the very variable standards of medical expertise in doctors and midwives. For obvious reasons, these problems were most keenly felt by the poor, but no family was safe from the threat of infant mortality.

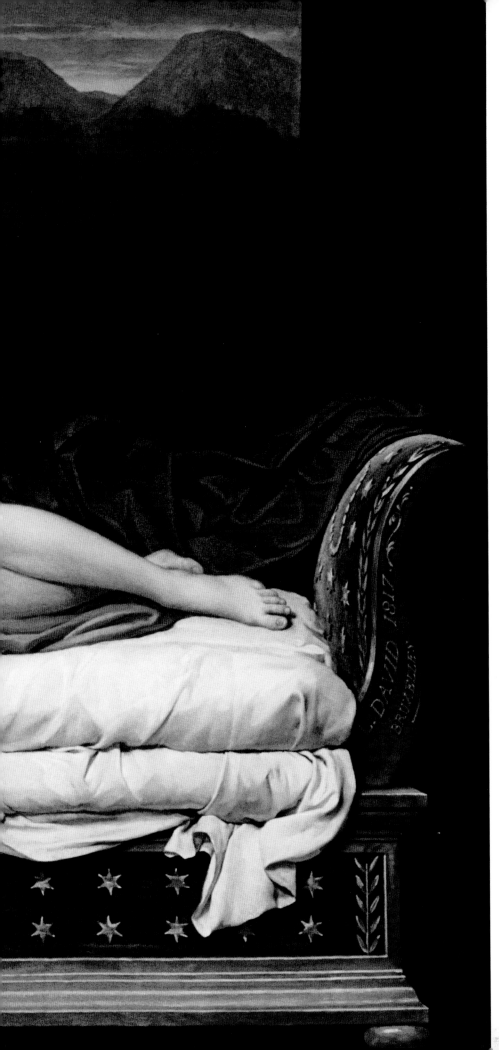

Cupid and Classical Figures

According to Hesiod (active *c.* 700 BC) Eros was one of the most ancient, primeval gods, the son of Chaos. It was only in the later Greek myths that he became identified as the son of Aphrodite, the goddess of love. His Roman equivalent was Cupid, son of Venus. Eros was portrayed on Greek vases and sculpture, usually as a youth. In Roman times cupids were sometimes included on funerary sculpture, and it was these images which early Christian artists transformed into angels.

Cupid became a common sight in later Western art, though often in a supporting role. His most popular theme was the romance with Psyche, which stemmed from an anecdote in *The Golden Ass* by Apuleius (*fl. c.* AD 155). This was a fairy tale rather than a bona fide legend, although Renaissance philosophers turned it into an allegory of the soul. Aside from this Cupid appeared mainly as an attendant of Venus or, in a variety of light-hearted domestic escapades, as an impish child. He was also used as a symbol of love in numerous allegories. The most ubiquitous of these showed him wearing a blindfold, to signify that 'love is blind'. Increasingly, he became just a piece of ornamental flummery, indistinguishable from the cherubs in religious art.

Cupid and Psyche, 1817
by Jacques-Louis David (1748–1825)

David's picture illustrates an early episode in the romance of Cupid and Psyche (*see* page 162). The god of love is infatuated with the girl, but is still keeping his identity a secret from her. He rises from his bed just as dawn is breaking, so that he can slip away before she awakes. His usual attributes, his bow and arrow, are in easy reach, while Psyche can be identified by her traditional symbol, the butterfly (*see* pages 164–65). A live one flutters above her head, while a second is prominently displayed on the front of the couch.

Looking at this piece of bland eroticism it is hard to believe that David had once been the greatest political artist of his age. His impassioned depictions of Roman virtue and self-sacrifice had helped to build up the momentum of the French Revolution (1789), and he himself had played a part in the new government, almost ending up on the guillotine as a result.

Putto Sur Un Monstre Marin ('Cupid on a Sea Monster'), c. 1857
by William Adolphe Bouguereau (1825–1905)

Cherubs became associated with the sea through their links with Venus. The goddess of love was born out of the sea, and it became commonplace to use putti as decorative accessories in depictions of this event. After a time, the putti began to appear on their own in maritime subjects. Early cartographers, for example, would sometimes adorn their maps with them since this helped to fill out a space in their charts that might otherwise seem rather dull and empty. Normally, however, the cherub's mount was a dolphin since this also had associations with Venus.

In Bouguereau's picture, the goat-headed creature refers to a baser kind of love. Since antiquity the goat had been a traditional symbol of lust, linked with Pan and the lecherous, drunken antics of the satyrs. In Christian art, by contrast, it was associated with the damned. This particular creature also bears a resemblance to the astrological symbol for Capricorn, which consists of a goat's head and body, combined with a spiralling, serpent-like tail. In the nineteenth century this was occasionally used in allegories of the 12 months, where it represented December, or the four seasons, where it signified winter.

Eros, 1876
by Jacques-Clément Wagrez (1846–1908)

By the latter part of the nineteenth century, depictions of Cupid or Eros had often become cloyingly sentimental. This painting by Wagrez, however, captures the spirit of the ancient deity. Eros is portrayed as a mischievous youth taking pot shots at passers-by who come within his range. The relaxed pose emphasizes that as far as he is concerned, he is engaged in a game, rather than a serious piece of marksmanship. The victims are chosen at random and, like any irresponsible child, Eros takes no interest in the serious effects that his arrows may cause.

For the Greeks, this behaviour mirrored the cruel and unpredictable nature of lust itself. Accordingly the earliest depictions of the deity portrayed him as a Ker, a winged 'Spite'. In this guise he was bracketed alongside other banes of human existence such as sickness and old age. During the Renaissance he was often shown blindfolded. For some

commentators this referred to the randomness of Cupid's targets, while also underlining the 'blind' or irrational behaviour that could ensue when someone fell in love. Others conversely saw it as an illustration of spiritual love. Hence Shakespeare's remark, 'Love looks not with the eyes, but with the mind;/And therefore is wing'd Cupid painted blind'.

Love and the Maiden, 1877
by John Roddam Spencer Stanhope (1829–1908)

Throughout his career, Stanhope was closely associated with the Pre-Raphaelite circle. He helped paint the murals in the Oxford Union, he had a studio next to Rossetti and he was a lifelong friend of Burne-Jones. He also shared their interests, most notably their devotion to early Italian art. This picture, for example, has affinities with Botticelli's (c. 1445–1510) *Primavera*. The dancers in the background are reminiscent of the Graces, while the profusion of flowers helps to conjure up a dreamlike atmosphere.

Stylistically Stanhope was chiefly influenced by Burne-Jones. His figures have the same pale, languid air. He also followed the latter's experiments with 'subjectless' paintings, paintings that evoked a mood rather than a specific storyline. In this instance, Stanhope appears to be depicting a scene from a Classical legend or a literary source, but neither of these is clearly identified. The title is deliberately vague. Instead the artist offers his public the suggestion of a romance: a young woman has apparently been struck by one of Cupid's arrows and gazes up adoringly at the love god, while he hurries off, seemingly oblivious to her. From these bare elements the spectator must use their imagination to create their own narrative.

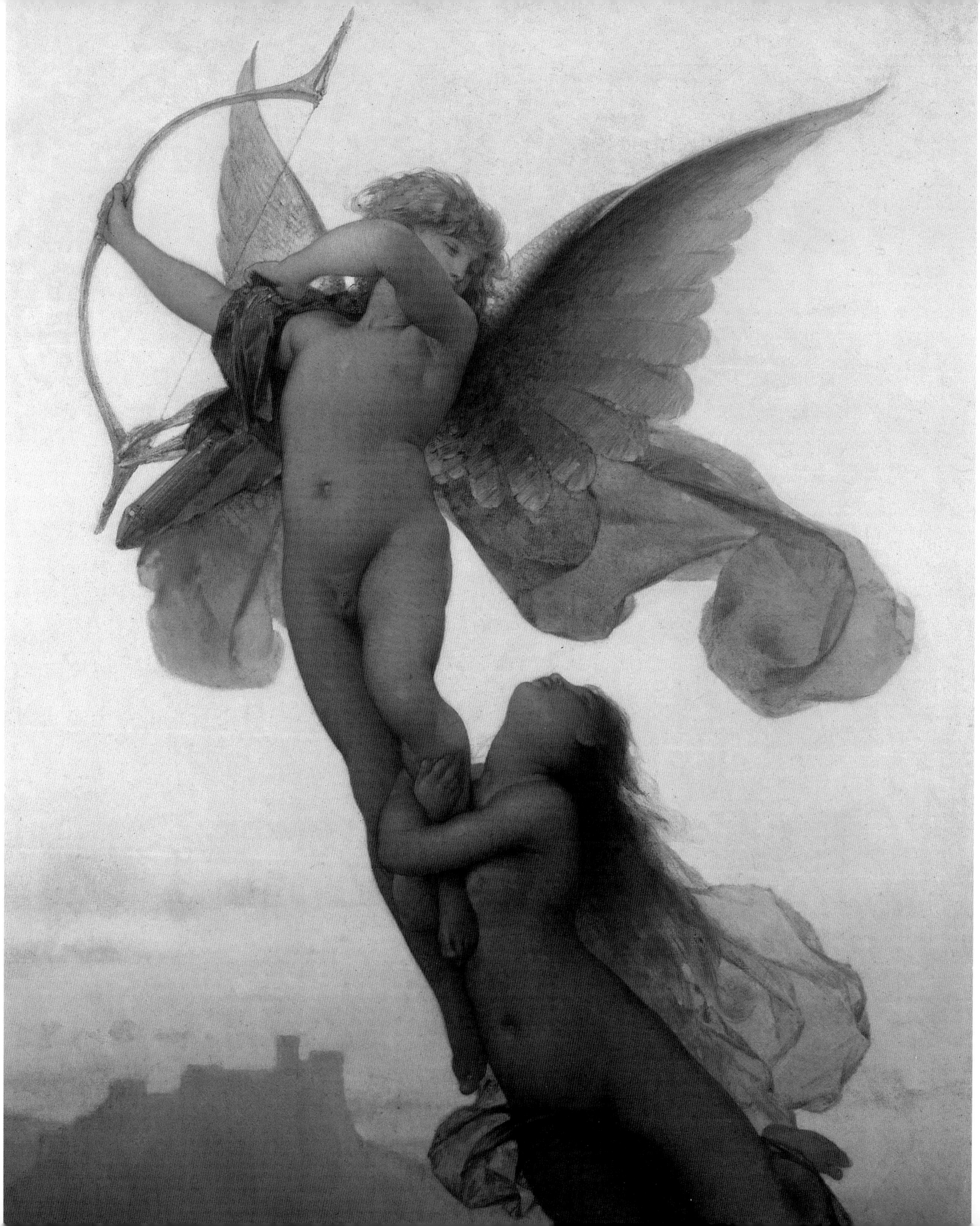

L'Amour et Psyche ('Cupid and Psyche'), 1878
by Eugène Medard (1847–87)

This tangled tale revolved around Psyche, a young maiden whose beauty won her great renown. It even aroused the jealousy of Venus, who sent her son, Cupid, to unleash one of his arrows at the girl so that she would become infatuated with some hideous creature. This cruel plot backfired, however, and Cupid himself fell in love with her. He installed Psyche in his palace and came to her chamber every night under cover of darkness. He also forbade her to try and look upon his face. Psyche soon fell under the spell of this mysterious stranger, but was fearful of his insistence on secrecy. Eventually her curiosity got the better of her and she lit her lamp. Unfortunately a drop of hot oil fell on Cupid's skin, waking him instantly. He was furious at her disobedience and immediately flew off. Here Medard illustrates her vain attempt to hold him back.

Because of its ancient origins, most artists tended to depict this story in a Classical manner, laying particular emphasis on the study of the nude form. This version, however, is more akin to the Romantic fantasies about knights and damsels. Even the silhouette of Cupid's palace resembles a medieval castle.

Cupid's Arrows, 1882
by Léon Jean Basile Perrault (1832–1908)

From an early stage, Cupid was traditionally depicted with a bow and a quiver of arrows. The latter had long been used to represent any unseen phenomenon that struck out of the blue. In particular, arrows were linked with sickness and the plague. Cupid's weapons also denoted strength. Artists sometimes showed the young deity carving his bow out of one of Hercules' clubs. This was meant to emphasize the overwhelming power of love.

Cupid's bow and arrow were first mentioned by Euripides (c. 485–406 BC), and later Ovid (43 BC–17 AD) specified in his *Metamorphoses* that the god employed two different types of arrow. The better-known variety, which kindled love, was made out of gold, but on rare occasions he also made use of lead arrows, which produced the opposite effect. These featured in the myth of Daphne and Apollo. Foolishly, the latter once teased Cupid for playing with weapons that were better suited to a grown warrior. The

youngster took his revenge by shooting a golden arrow into Apollo and a lead one into the object of his affections, a nymph called Daphne. She was so repulsed by the deity that she begged to be turned into a tree, rather than submit to Apollo's embraces.

Cupid and Psyche, c. 1889
after William Adolphe Bouguereau (1825–1905)

The image on this ceramic plaque was based on a painting by the French academic artist, William Bouguereau. In the original design the figures were shown full length. Significantly, there is a difference in the children's wings. Cupid has conventional angelic plumage, while his companion has butterfly wings. This illustrates the dual nature of her character.

According to the ancient tale, Psyche was human and in paintings that remained faithful to the narrative she was usually portrayed without wings. However, for Renaissance humanists her story also served as an allegory for the soul's journey through life (her name is the Greek word for 'soul'). As a result she acquired some of its visual attributes. On ancient sarcophagi (stone tombs) the soul had sometimes been represented as a butterfly emerging from a chrysalis. Later it was depicted as a tiny, winged human figure. These concepts are combined in Bouguereau's picture.

Given the sexual nature of the story, it is unusual to find Cupid and Psyche portrayed as children. However, Bouguereau was probably illustrating the end of their tale when, after many tribulations, they were finally reunited in the afterlife. In this context the infants may symbolize the innocence and purity of their heavenly existence.

L'Amour Mouillé, 1890
by William Adolphe Bouguereau (1825–1905)

Like Peter Pan, Cupid never grew up. Even though some of the stories associated with him have a fairly adult theme – the legend of Cupid and Psyche is an obvious example – he was increasingly portrayed as a young child. By the nineteenth century there was also a growing tendency to use Classical accessories as nothing more than decorative trappings. Here, for example, there is no obvious story line. The artist simply wanted to produce an attractive picture of a youngster.

The idealization of children in art and literature went hand in hand with a growing interest in their welfare. The Industrial Revolution brought with it a dependency on child labour, particularly in the mines and the cotton mills. Attempts were made to redress this situation in the early Victorian period. One of the principal reformers was the seventh Earl of Shaftesbury (1801–85), who was instrumental in passing the Factory Acts

(1833–50) and the Mines Act (1842), which restricted the employment of children. Fittingly, when a monument was created in his honour, it took the form of a statue of Eros, the name for the Greek god that the Romans later referred to as Cupid. This famous landmark is situated next to Shaftesbury Avenue in London, the street that was named after him.

Le Sauvetage ('The Rescue'), 1894
by Emile Munier (1840–95)

Sentimental pictures of young children were extremely popular in the late-nineteenth century, whether in a domestic setting or in the guise of figures from the past. Here, two youngsters are portrayed as mischievous cupids. They have been larking about near the river and a quiver of arrows has fallen in the water. A second quiver is visible at the left-hand side of the picture.

Munier's father was an upholsterer and at the start of his career Emile followed a similar path, working at the Gobelins, a famous tapestry factory. He switched to painting after becoming interested in the work of François Boucher (1703–70), a Rococo artist who had produced designs for the Gobelins. He was also inspired by the example of William Adolphe Bouguereau (1825–1905), who became his friend and mentor. The latter nicknamed him 'sage Munier' ('Munier the wise'). He adopted the same highly polished style as Bouguereau, although his subject matter was quite different – by the 1880s he was specializing in paintings of children and animals. Munier's two children, Henri and Marie-Louise, served as models for many of these pictures. His most successful work in this vein was *Three Friends*, featuring a child, a kitten and a dog, which became famous after Pears Soap used it in one of their advertising campaigns.

Love Disarmed, 1889
by Will Hicok Low (1853–1932)

When artists painted Cupid, they usually focused on his role as the god of love or on the story with Psyche. From the Renaissance onwards though, he was also portrayed as a mischievous young lad in a variety of light-hearted scenes. The Education of Cupid and the Punishment of Cupid were particularly popular themes. Low's painting falls into the latter category. The young deity has been causing havoc with his bow and arrow, so his mother (Venus) has confiscated them. He points pleadingly at the arrow, but it is not returned. The subject also carries playful echoes of pictures of Venus disarming her lover, Mars (the god of war). These carried such titles as *The Triumph of Love* or *Love Overcoming Strife* and were often commissioned as wedding presents.

It is scarcely surprising that Low chose to depict a classical subject of this kind. Although American by birth, he trained in Paris under two leading academic artists, Jean-Léon Gérôme (1824–1904) and Carolus-Duran (1837–1917), who both produced work in this vein. On his return to the United States, Low made his mark in a rather different field, becoming a notable decorative artist. He designed ornamental panels for the Waldorf-Astoria Hotel in New York, as well as a number of stained-glass windows for churches.

L'Innocence, 1890
by William Adolphe Bouguereau (1825–1905)

Towards the end of the nineteenth century there was a vogue for portraying allegorical pictures of young women. In most cases artists preferred to depict the most extreme forms of behaviour. Either the women were paragons of virtue, as in this case, or they were manifestations of evil, represented by a femme fatale. Here, the subject is Innocence. Her purity is symbolized by her white dress. She also resists temptation by ignoring the two cherubs, who are trying to whisper thoughts of love into her ears.

In many ways, Bouguereau was the archetypal establishment figure in the French art world. He won the Prix de Rome in 1850, the award most coveted by young academic artists, and for almost 30 years (1876–1905) he was on the governing body of the Académie des Beaux-Arts. This institution had enormous influence, organizing the exhibitions at the Salon, supervising education and advising on state commissions. By reputation it was fiercely conservative, opposing the Impressionists and most other avant-garde trends. Paul Cézanne (1839–1906), for example, expressed his regret at being barred from the 'Salon of Monsieur Bouguereau'.

The Uninvited Guest, 1906
by Eleanor Fortescue Brickdale (1871–1945)

This sumptuous painting is a moral fable in medieval dress, precisely the type of subject that appealed to the Pre-Raphaelites and their followers. A wedding has just taken place and the bridal pair are now proceeding out of the church. As they do so, they pass the 'Uninvited Guest', the figure of Love who sits forlornly on the bare earth. The marriage is not a love match. This is emphasized by the arrow lying on the ground. Cupid has taken it out of his quiver, but has not used it. Instead, the fine clothes and the noble bearing of the guests suggest that the motives of the couple are governed by money or status. Love looks reprovingly at the newlyweds. He could still fire his arrow, of course, but there are hints that he will not. Already the bride's gown has become snagged on some brambles, suggesting that the course of her marriage may not run smoothly.

Brickdale's painting is notable for the immaculate depiction of the satin gown, and more so for the portrayal of Love. This figure bears all the attributes of Cupid, but is far removed from the usual mischievous boy. He is older and more thoughtful, aware of the consequences of love and of its absence.

The Love Letter
by Gabriel-Joseph-Marie-Augustin Ferrier (1847–1914)

The writing and receiving of love letters had long been a popular theme for artists. For the moneyed classes, marriage was still essentially a business arrangement with considerations of wealth and status taking priority over romance. Letters, even love letters, could come under parental scrutiny and during the Victorian era chaperones proved an added restriction. Even after the advent of bicycles, which seemed to offer young people a new sense of liberty, in 1896, a Chaperone Cyclists' Association was founded.

Many nineteenth-century artists preferred to portray this type of subject as a contemporary issue, but Ferrier's picture has a deliberately archaic feel, typified by the old-fashioned quill pen and the cherub who peers over the woman's shoulder. This kind of image was frequently reproduced on prints and postcards. The latter were still a novelty, and many young girls made a hobby of collecting them. As one journalist noted: 'Young ladies, who have escaped the philatelic intention or wearied of collecting Christmas cards, have been known to fill albums with missives of this kind'. The popularity of romantic cards increased during the First World War, when women sent them to their sweethearts at the Front.

The Wings of Desire
by Guillaume Seignac (1870–1924)

When humanist philosophers wrote about Cupid and Psyche, they described them as an allegory of the union between Desire (Cupid) and the Soul (Psyche), which produced Pleasure as its offspring. In artistic terms, the status of Cupid was often downgraded. Venus was seen as the presiding deity of love and he was cast in the role of her son or one of her attendants. This role is emphasized here by the red roses that adorn his hair. These blooms were sacred to Venus and were one of her chief attributes. This stems from the legend that the first red rose was created when she pricked her foot on a thorn and stained a white rose crimson with her blood.

In the nineteenth century, the theme of Cupid was often a pretext for portraying a pretty child or to celebrate childhood. Children featured heavily in the novels of Charles Dickens (1812–70) and Mark Twain (1835–1910), while artists illustrated scenes from their everyday lives. Sentimental images such as this were often reproduced and hung in the family home.

The Passing of Venus (copy of tapestry),
1923–26
by John Henry Dearle, after Burne-Jones
(Dearle 1860–1932)

This is a variant on the theme of the Triumph of Venus. On the left, the goddess of love sits enthroned in her winged chariot while Cupid carries out her bidding. As he draws his bow the women on the right shrink back in fear. The maiden lying prostrate beneath his feet, together with the three on the left, have already felt the force of the arrows of love.

Sir Edward Coley Burne-Jones produced the basic design for this tapestry, although it was still incomplete at the time of his death in 1898. He had been a crucial figure within William Morris's (1834–96) firm, Morris & Co., for many years. After his demise many of his duties were taken on by John Dearle, who had started out as an apprentice with the company and eventually became its managing director. He adapted Burne-Jones's design and supervised the first weaving of the tapestry at Merton Abbey, between 1901 and 1907. This version of the tapestry was destroyed by fire in 1910 at an exhibition in Brussels. Fortunately a colour photograph had been taken, and from this source Dearle was able to produce a copy when a reproduction was commissioned by George Booth, the publisher of the Detroit News. In 1927 Booth donated this to the Detroit Institute of Art.

Love and Time, date unknown
by John Melhuish Strudwick (1849–1937)

Strudwick was one of a sizeable group of fin de siècle artists who became followers of Burne-Jones, sharing his taste for slender, languid figures and enigmatic subject matter. Those qualities are in evidence in this picture, which belongs to a series of allegories relating to Time. These were suffused with an air of gentle melancholy. In some of the pictures, Time was represented in the conventional manner, as an old man with a scythe, but Strudwick also made use of a female figure who represented the Passing Hour.

Strudwick was trained at South Kensington and the Royal Academy Schools, though the results were not encouraging. He did begin to make progress, however, after becoming a studio assistant. Initially he was an assistant to John Spencer Stanhope (1829–1908), before moving on to join Burne-Jones. Strudwick showed only one picture at the Royal Academy. Like his mentor, he preferred to exhibit at the Grosvenor Gallery and the New Gallery. When interviewed by George Bernard Shaw (1856–1950) he confessed that he 'could not draw – never could'. Even so this did not prevent him from developing an elegant and nostalgic manner, which contemporaries described as Italianate; a considerable irony, given that he never visited the country.

The Stranger, 1902
by William Henry Margetson (1861–1940)

This type of study became popular in the late nineteenth century, when there was a taste for pictures that hinted at a story but did not offer a firm narrative. Here a woman sits in a reflective mood with Cupid at her feet. She is so wrapped up in her thoughts that she has lost interest in her book and does not appear to notice the god of love as he offers her a rose. By ignoring Cupid's gift there is a suggestion that she is the stranger in the title, a stranger to love.

Margetson studied at the South Kensington Schools and the Royal Academy, where he began exhibiting in 1885. He specialized in rather wistful studies of women on their own, usually cast in a vaguely allegorical or mythological setting. Some of these were adapted for use as advertising posters. He also produced a few religious pictures, most notably *Saint Mary at the Loom*.

Love in Idleness, date unknown
by Sidney Harold Meteyard (1868–1947)

Meteyard's depiction of Cupid marks a significant departure from the Victorian norm. In place of the customary pretty infant he portrays the deity as a sulky teenager reclining lazily on a couch, with his bow and arrows deposited untidily on the floor. In fact, the painting is an elaborate pun, as love-in-idleness is also the popular name of a plant, also known as the pansy. This flower was closely associated with Cupid. In *A Midsummer Night's Dream*, Oberon instructed Puck to seek it out, because it had magical properties. When its juice was sprinkled on the eyelids of someone who was asleep, it would cause them to dote on the first person they saw after they awoke. The pansy had acquired this power after one of Cupid's arrows missed its target and struck it. As Oberon explained:

Yet marked I where the bolt of Cupid fell: / It fell upon a little western flower,
Before, milk-white; now purple with love's wound: /
And maidens call it 'love-in-idleness'.

Fittingly, Cupid's wings are painted a sumptuous shade of purple.

Venus and Putti, 1768
by Nöel Hallé (1711–81)

The French painter Nöel Hallé depicts Venus, the goddess of love and fertility lying on a celestial cloud with two cherubic putti (Latin *putus* 'a little man'). The tiny putti are naked except for their wings. One putto to the right lies on his back playing with a pair of white doves, which are recognized as an attribute of Venus. The doves are touching their beaks as if to kiss each other. The putto on the left has thrown down his quiver of arrows (an attribute of Cupid), and embraces Venus, caressing her and kissing her. Venus lies back, enjoying the attention. Her kiss is sisterly or maternal, depicted as a brief caress of lips meeting. Winged putti are also referred to as *Amoretto* (from the Latin word *amore*, which means love, and can also refer to Cupid, the god of Love). In the Renaissance Cupid would be depicted as a winged youth, later changing to a chubby infant in the Baroque and Rococo era, as shown here.

Nöel Hallé was a successful painter, draughtsman and printmaker of Paris, winning the Prix de Rome in 1736. His style is typical of the period but he was equally capable of producing religious or mythological scenes, or architectural landscapes.

The Toilet of Venus, date unknown
by Constantin Makowsky (1839–1915)

This subject had been in circulation since the Renaissance, becoming particularly popular in Venice. It survived into the nineteenth century largely because the subject matter was so vague. It was not attached to any specific story from mythology, so artists tended to use it as a pretext for producing a decorative picture of a female nude. Traditionally in a *Toilet of Venus*, the nude was shown reclining, but in Makowsky's version the goddess is enthroned, a pose normally reserved for a *Triumph of Venus*.

The goddess is accompanied by several of her attributes. The most common of these is the mirror, a conventional symbol for vanity or lust. In Renaissance allegories Venus was often portrayed as a personification of lust, although later artists preferred to link her with *voluptas* or 'pleasure'. As usual she is surrounded by amoretti (the diminutive form of *amor* or 'love'), and these chubby figures act as playful reminders of the identity of the goddess. Amidst the profusion of flowers there are many roses, a plant that was sacred to Venus. The inclusion of a peacock in such a prominent position is a surprise, since the bird was traditionally associated with the goddess Juno. Here it may represent Pride.

The Birth of Venus, date unknown
by Hans Zatzka (1859–1945)

In Zatzka's playful scene, Love is personified by the goddess Venus. She was traditionally associated with the scallop shell as a result of the legend that she was born out of the sea and carried ashore on a giant shell. Many artists portrayed this subject, most famously Botticelli (*c.* 1445–1510) in his *Birth of Venus* (*c.* 1485), and some also depicted the shell as a type of boat drawn by swans. Here Zatzka has turned it into a bed, transforming the surrounding riverside scene into a romantic, open-air boudoir. Venus is surrounded by some of her traditional attributes. Roses are scattered everywhere, referring to the myth that she helped create the first red rose. Similarly the profusion of other flowers relates to the legend that after she first set foot on dry land, flowers sprang up in her footsteps. The frolicking putti, who hover in the air, are also a predictable feature. Only the fairy strikes an incongruous note. Fairy painting was very much an English tradition, which had little impact on the other side of the Channel. When they were included in French pictures, fairies were often used rather indiscriminately as a general fantasy element in any mythical scene. (*See* also another similar work by Zatzka – *Springtime* – on the front cover of this book.)

The Birth of Venus, 1863
by Alexandre Cabanel (1823–89)

According to legend, the goddess of love rose fully formed out of the sea. In some versions of the myth she was wafted ashore on a giant scallop shell, while others reported that she sprang from the foam itself. This foam had gathered around the castrated genitals of Uranus (the personification of heaven), which had been flung into the sea. The Greek equivalent of Venus, the goddess Aphrodite, took her name from the word for 'foam' (aphros). Cabanel exploited the erotic potential of this theme to the full. His Venus reclines seductively, as if she were in the boudoir rather than the sea.

The fate of Cabanel's picture offers a telling lesson on the fickle nature of fame. In 1863 when it was exhibited at the Paris Salon it was the hit of the show. While paintings by Edouard Manet (1832–83), Paul Cézanne (1839–1906) and James McNeill Whistler (1834–1903) were rejected from the exhibition, it received a rapturous reception from both public and critics alike. It even found a distinguished buyer, Napoleon III himself. When he fell from power, however, it was passed to the Louvre. There, after a time, it fell out of fashion and was consigned to the storeroom.

Mercury, date unknown
Marcantonio Raimondi (c. 1480–1527/34)

When Christian artists came to depict angels, they drew inspiration from a number of classical deities, though the closest links were with Mercury. In addition to his winged apparel, he usually carried a herald's trumpet – as did many angels – or his *caduceus*. This was a winged staff entwined with serpents, which symbolized his role as a messenger of the gods. This was unquestionably a pagan emblem, but it can be found in some early depictions of Saint Michael.

There was an even closer link between Mercury and the archangel. Both became associated with the dead. Mercury was responsible for leading the deceased to the underworld and, like Saint Michael, he weighed their souls in a pair of scales. Michael is often portrayed with this attribute, particularly in scenes of the Last Judgement (*see* pages 87 and 105–09). It is clear that the archangel inherited this aspect of his role from the pagan deity. Significantly, a number of churches dedicated to the saint were founded on hilltop locations, which had previously been the site of temples devoted to Mercury.

Marcantonio Raimondi was an influential engraver, who helped to popularize the work of other Renaissance artists. His style was closely modelled on that of Albrecht Dürer (1471–1528) – so closely, in fact, that the German sued him for plagiarism.

PARIS AND MERCURY, 1597–1600
by ANNIBALE CARRACCI (1560–1609)

When Christian artists were painting angels they sometimes drew inspiration from the flying figures that appeared in Greek and Roman mythology. Images of Mercury, for example, were often used as a source. He did not actually have wings himself, though he was normally shown with winged sandals and a winged helmet, but the depiction of flight was the same in both cases. A simple comparison between Carracci's deity and the angel in Allori's *Allegory of Life* (*see* pages 186–87) can confirm that the two figures were treated in a very similar way.

Mercury also performed the same kind of role as an angel, acting as an intermediary between god and humanity. In this particular scene he is following the orders of his father, Jupiter, by taking the golden apple of Discord to Paris. He also passes on a message to Paris, instructing him to give the apple to the fairest of three goddesses – Juno, Minerva and Venus. This fateful beauty contest will eventually lead to the Trojan War.

Paris and Mercury forms part of Carracci's masterpiece, the decoration of the ceiling in the Farnese Palace in Rome. The frescoes, illustrating the loves of the gods, were executed in the Gallery, where Cardinal Farnese kept his collection of antique sculpture.

Allegorical Figures

When Early Christian artists began to search around for ways of depicting angels, they found a wealth of inspiration in ancient art. The Greeks and Romans, in particular, used winged figures to personify a bewildering variety of abstract qualities and concepts. These included such things as Peace, Fortune, Sleep, Death, History, Night and Melancholy. The most influential, by far, were Fame and Victory, since their attributes – a trumpet and a sword, respectively – were also used by angels. By the Renaissance, this list had grown still longer. Father Time acquired wings during this period, while the depiction of Poverty as a winged hand dates from the Middle Ages. As time went on, the artistic influences worked both ways, as painters of allegories looked for inspiration in pictures of angels.

The use of winged allegorical figures continued well into the twentieth century. It enjoyed a huge surge of popularity during the Great War, when illustrators looked to the past for inspiration. Recruiting posters and notices concerning the war effort were emblazoned with updated versions of Victory; postcards sent to loved ones at the front showed militant angels standing shoulder to shoulder with servicemen; finally, when the carnage was over, the figure of Peace was featured on tombs and war memorials.

Allegory of Life, *c.* 1555–1607
by Alessandro Allori (1535–1607)

Most of the angels in heaven produced sweet, celestial music, but some could produce noises that were far less welcome. On the final day, some will be despatched with their horns, to sound the last trump. Their deafening blast will wake the dead from their graves and lead them to judgement: 'for the trumpet shall sound, and the dead shall be raised incorruptible, and we shall be changed' (1 Corinthians 15:52).

This is the fate that has befallen the central figure in Allori's gloomy allegory. The man is surrounded by episodes from his past life, which include scenes of lust, drunkenness and violence. He clings on desperately to a globe, which represents his earthly life. But death takes that away and now he is confronted by the angel with the trumpet, calling him to judgement.

Alessandro Allori (1535–1607) was a Florentine painter, the adopted son of Agnolo Bronzino (1503–72). From his example, Allori developed a graceful Mannerist style that brought him considerable success. He was also strongly influenced by Michelangelo (1475–1564), as is evident from his masterpiece, *The Pearl Fishers* (1570–71). His son, Cristofano (1577–1621), also became a painter.

Peter the Great and the Battle of Poltava, after 1709 (Battle of Poltava)
attributed to Gottfried Danhauer (*c.* 1680–1733/7)

This is an allegorical portrait of Peter the Great (1672–1725), the celebrated Russian ruler who transformed his homeland into a major European power. The artist has depicted him against the backdrop of one of his greatest achievements, the victory at the Battle of Poltava (1709), where Russian forces overcame the Swedish army. Peter's success in this conflict was crucial as it effectively ended the invaders' attempts to capture the Ukraine. Danhauer has also added the winged figure of Fame swooping down from the clouds to crown Peter's victory.

The personification of Fame as an airborne female figure dates back to classical times. She was often portrayed on tomb sculpture commemorating the actions of dead heroes. In this context she was often shown with a crown or a palm frond, both of which were conventional symbols of victory. The trumpet was a later development, which came to the fore during the

Renaissance. The instrument was long and straight, reminiscent of the trumpets blown by angels on the Day of Judgement as well as the herald's trumpet carried by Mercury. In some allegorical pictures Fame carried two instruments symbolizing different types of fame. One of these echoed the sweet sound of success, while the other – usually a shorter, more raucous horn – was a token of ill repute.

Time Unveiling Truth, 1733
by Jean-François de Troy (1679–1752)

This type of allegory was extremely popular during the Baroque era. In the centre, Time reveals Truth, confirming the old maxim that 'the truth will out'. At the same time, Truth is unmasking the figure of Fraud, who sits on her left. These proceedings are witnessed approvingly by the Four Cardinal Virtues, who can be seen on the left. They are Temperance, Justice, Fortitude and Prudence, each of whom can be identified by their traditional attributes.

The notion of Father Time can be traced back to antiquity, although some of his symbols were acquired by accident. The Greeks muddled up the word for 'time' (*chronos*) with an aged, agricultural god called Cronus. As a result, they began to portray Time as an old man with a scythe. The wings were added by Renaissance artists, who wanted to convey the idea that time goes quickly. The idea of depicting Truth with a nude figure also derived from antiquity. This seemed an admirable way of demonstrating that the truth should be unadorned. In many cases, Truth was also shown with a globe beneath her feet. This indicated that she was above the mundane concerns of earthly existence.

Cupids: Allegory of Painting, eighteenth century
by François Boucher (1703–70)

From the Counter Reformation onwards, cherubs began to proliferate in art. At first they were mainly confined to religious paintings, as examples of the heavenly host, but gradually they were put to more generalized, decorative uses.

This trend reached a peak in the work of François Boucher (1703–70), who was the leading exponent of the Rococo style. He introduced his chubby infants into a wide variety of themes, ranging from mythologies and allegories to historical scenes and portraits. In all of these his approach was playful and light-hearted. Allegories, for instance, could often be ponderous affairs, but this canvas exudes charm. There are no complex ideas or obscure symbols, just a simple picture of two little boys trying to draw, while the statue of a woman's head appears to look on with a benign, maternal expression. Boucher's mythological scenes were in a similar vein. In a typical example he showed a group of putti holding up a target with a heart on it, so that Cupid could practise his archery skills.

Boucher's decorative instincts were enhanced by his work in other fields: he often translated his images onto tapestries and ceramics for instance.

Horatius Cocles crowned by Victory, eighteenth century
by an unknown artist

In ancient classical art the winged figure of Victory (Nike) was portrayed in many different guises. She could be shown with her hand cupped to her mouth, announcing the name of the person or the event that she was commemorating; she could equally be depicted riding a chariot or assembling a military trophy. In her most common pose though, she rewarded a victor by crowning him or her with a laurel wreath. The recipient might be a warrior, but could just as easily be the winner of an athletics competition or a poetry contest.

Horatius Cocles was a legendary Roman soldier who was said to have won a heroic victory against the Etruscans in the sixth century BC. According to the accounts of Plutarch (c. 46–c. 120 AD) and Livy (59 BC–17 AD) he defended the bridge across the Tiber single-handedly, before swimming to safety. Cocles' mythical exploits have provided inspiration for many artists, including a celebrated version by Charles Le Brun (1619–90). Thomas Macaulay (1800–59) also chose it for one of his *Lays of Ancient Rome* (1842).

My Soul is an Enchanted Boat, c. 1875
by Walter Crane (1845–1915)

Crane painted this atmospheric picture near the start of his career, when he was closely involved with the Pre-Raphaelite circle. He admired the air of romantic mystery that they managed to achieve in their pictures. In particular, he was impressed by the poetic fantasies of Burne-Jones and described the effect of seeing his work for the first time: 'The curtain had been lifted and we had a glimpse into… a twilight world of dark mysterious woodland, haunted streams, meads of dark green starred with burning flowers, veiled in a dim and mystic light…'. A winged figure was a conventional symbol for the soul, but usually it was tiny; sometimes it was an infant. More importantly it was always shown with the human in question, often issuing from their mouth at the time of death. Crane's lyrical vision marks a new departure, in which the river provides a satisfying metaphor for the soul's journey through life. His inspiration probably came from two Arthurian themes, which were popular with the Pre-Raphaelites and their followers. One of these was the tragic tale of the Lady of Shalott, who was often depicted in a boat. The other concerned the death of Arthur, when the hero was conveyed to Avalon in a fairy vessel.

Peace, date unknown
by Ludwig Knaus (1829–1910)

Here again is an image of a figure whose wings, rather than signify angelic status, serve to represent an abstract concept simply by underlining the point that the figure is not a human being. Traditionally, Peace was symbolized by a winged woman wearing an olive crown. She is often depicted, as here, with a *cornucopia* ('horn of plenty'). The idea of this was to emphasize the material benefits that would follow when peace was agreed. The addition of the putti, gathering up the flowers, is an unusual touch. Knaus probably included them for decorative reasons, although they are also associated with roses, which are among the blooms that Peace is scattering. Coincidentally, there is also a rose called 'Peace'. Winged female figures were used to represent a variety of other subjects; ironically, the closest parallel is probably the personification of Victory.

Born in Wiesbaden, Knaus was trained in Dusseldorf and Paris. He lived in Italy for a time, but returned to Germany to become a professor at the Berlin Academy. He was principally known as a genre painter and as one of the leading lights of the Dusseldorf school.

In Terris Pax Hominibus Bonae Voluntatis, 1904
Artist unknown

The title of this illustration is taken partly from '*Gloria in Altissimis Deo, et in Terra Pax, Hominibus Bonae Voluntatis*' – 'Glory to God in the Highest, and on Earth peace and goodwill towards men' (Luke 2:14). This announcement is made by an angel, a messenger from God, to shepherds in the fields, watching over their flocks, near Bethlehem during the Nativity. The angel announces the news of the infant Christ's birth and urges the shepherds to visit him in the stable nearby. The angel tells them of the great joy that has come to Earth. The words of the title praise God in the language of the angels. Saint Luke is an Evangelist; he spreads the word of God in the most pleasing terms.

The words of the biblical reference run along the bottom of the illustration. At the centre, in half portrait an angel has eyes closed, in contemplation of the wondrous news that he/she brings to people on Earth. The wings are outspread, the hands clasped in prayer. The hair of the angel is of burnished golden red. The background of gold crescent moon and a plethora of stars are accentuated by the deep turquoise colour on which they are depicted. This is a typical work of the Arts and Crafts period.

Share in the Victory, c. 1918
by William Haskell Coffin (1878–1941)

During much of the First World War there was a profound distinction between the grim reality of conflict at the front and the image that was circulated back home. The experiences of those soldiers enduring the misery of the trenches was represented only in the contributions of the war poets. However, in the propaganda and the memorials, artists looked back nostalgically to a more comfortable and chivalrous view of war.

Many of the wartime images revolved around knights in armour, deliberately evoking memories of Agincourt or the Crusades. Coffin echoed this theme – one of his *War Savings Stamps* posters featured Joan of Arc – but in this example he went back even further. His depiction of Victory is barely distinguishable from the ancient sculptures of Nike (*see* page 14). As in the past, it is represented by a winged female figure, attired in classical drapery. She also carries Victory's traditional attributes: the sword, the laurel crown and the palm leaf. The origin of the laurel crown can be traced back to the Pythian Games, which were held at Delphi. There they were awarded to the winners of various sporting contests. Laurel crowns were also worn by Roman emperors when they took part in triumphal processions.

Angel at the Door, 1930
by Eleanor Fortescue Brickdale (1871–1945)

Brickdale painted both fairies and angels, frequently placing them in a medieval context or using them to illustrate a romantic tale. Here, an angel comes to the door of a rich household begging for alms. The occupant is so suspicious, however, that she only opens the door a little way. As a result she fails to notice the angel's wings, along with the crown in his hand.

During the nineteenth century and beyond, there was a ready market for paintings of children dressed up as beggars. The Victorians did not invent this kind of picture – Thomas Gainsborough (1727–88) and Sir Joshua Reynolds (1723–92) both produced pictures featuring similar ragamuffins, but it was the Victorians who embraced the subject with enthusiasm. Their street urchins were, in a sense, the urban equivalent of the eighteenth-century taste for dressing up as shepherds and shepherdesses. So when Lewis Carroll came to photograph Alice Liddell (the model for his *Alice in Wonderland*), he dressed her up as a beggar girl even though she came from a prosperous family.

Credits

All pictures courtesy of Corbis (including 91 © Yaroslav and Galina Dobrynine) except:

Sotheby's Picture Library: 5, 9, 46, 47 (© F. Pickford Marriott), 48–49, 50–51, 61, 116–17, 121, 122–23, 124, 126 (© Robert Burns), 132–33, 146–47, 148, 150–51, 155, 158, 159, 162–63, 164–65, 166, 170–71 (© Eleanor Fortescue Brickdale), 173, 174–75, 182, 183 (© Hans Zatzka), 192–93, 194, 197 (© Eleanor Fortescue Brickdale)

Christie's Images Ltd: 24, 25, 43, 44, 129, 131, 134–35, 149, 160–61, 167 (NYC), 169, 172, 176 (© John Melhuish Strudwick), 177 (© William Henry Margetson), 178 (© Sidney Harold Meteyard), 180–81

The Bridgeman Art Library: 130 (© The Fine Art Society, London, UK)

Author: Iain Zaczek was born in Dundee, Scotland, and educated at Wadham College, Oxford, and the Courtauld Institute of Art. He has since gone on to forge an impressive career as a freelance writer on art- and Celtic-related subjects, and is interested in particular in Pre-Raphaelite art and International Gothic. His publications include *Essential Art Deco* (Parragon, 2000), *The Essential William Morris* (Parragon, 1999), *The Art of the Icon* (Studio Editions, 1994), *Lovers in Art* (Studio Editions, 1994), *Impressionist Interiors* (Studio Editions, 1993) and *Fairy Art* (Star Fire, 2005).

Contributing author: Elizabeth Keevill was born in Norwich. She trained as a printmaker and textile designer at Camberwell School of Art and Crafts in London and at ENSAD in Paris and studied for a degree in art history and history with the Open University. She is a writer, journalist and broadcaster, specializing in art and design, and is co-author of *Dali*, also published by Flame Tree. Elizabeth lectures in the History of Art, Design and Architecture at Kingston University, Surrey. She lives in Surbiton with her husband Kevin and daughter Isabelle.

Contributing author: Ros Ormiston is a lecturer at Kingston University, Surrey, teaching History of Art, Design and Architecture. Specialist subjects include Classical Civilization, Renaissance Italy and Contemporary Architecture. She divides her time between London and Cumbria and Italy, writing features for academic journals and consumer publications. Previous books for Flame Tree Publishing include *The Colour Source Book* (2006) and *Alphonse Mucha: Masterworks* (2007)

INDEX

A

Abbey, Edwin Austin *Galahad Visited by an Angel* 129
Abraham 12, 14, 17, 19
Adam and Eve 21, 22, 24, 27, 28, 32, 37, 50
Albert Memorial 129
allegorical figures 186, 187, 189, 191, 193, 194, 195, 197
Allori, Alessandro *Allegory of Life* 184, 187
Allori, Cristofo 187
Amalteo, Pomponio *The Annunciation* 39
Andrea del Verrocchio *Tobias and the Angel* 29
Angel of Mons 124
Annunciation 32, 34, 37, 39, 40, 43, 44, 45, 46, 49, 50, 61
Anubis 13
Aphrodite 157, 182
Apocalypse 98
Apocalypse, fifthteenth century 105
Apocrypha 29, 46, 52, 62, 124
Apuleius *The Golden Ass* 157
Archangel Michael 88
archangels 10
    Gabriel 19, 32, 39, 40, 43, 44, 46, 50, 52
    Michael 86, 87, 88, 91, 93, 95, 98, 182
    Raphael 12, 27, 29, 31, 124
Arthur 118, 126, 127, 193
Arts and Crafts 194
Assumption 62, 65, 67, 69, 70
Assyria 10, 31, 120
    Winged Bull 12

B

Babb, John Staines *Adolescentiae Somnia Celestia* 132
Babylonia 12, 19, 24, 31, 120
Baroque 177, 191
Bates, Harry 129
Bernini, Gianlorenzo *Saint Teresa* 40, 115
Blair, Robert *The Grave* 101, 102
Blake, William 92
    Christ in the Sepulchre Guarded by Angels 79
    Death of the Good Old Man 101
    Meeting of a Family in Heaven 102
    Satan Arousing the Rebel Angels 96
Book of Daniel 19, 39, 91
Book of Exodus 44, 79
Book of Ezekiel 12, 110
Book of Genesis 14, 17, 21, 24, 98
Book of James 52
Book of Revelations 52, 86, 87, 91, 92, 95, 136
Book of Samuel 24
Book of Tobit 12, 29, 31, 124
Booth, George 173
Bosch, Hieronymus 95
Botticelli, Sandro 160, 181
    Annunciation 34, 39
    Coronation of the Virgin with Saints 62
    Madonna of the Pomegranate 61
    Mystic Nativity 52
Botticini, Francesco *The Assumption of the Virgin* 67
Boucher, François 166
    Cupids 191
Boughton, George Henry *The Vision at the Martyr's Well* 130
Bouguereau, William Adolphe 166
    Amour Mouillé 165
    Annunciation 46
    Cupid and Psyche 165
    Innocence 169
    Putto sur un Monstre Marin 159
Brickdale, Eleanor Fortescue
    Angel at the Door 197
    Uninvited Guest 169
Bronzino, Agnolo 187
Bruegel, Pieter the Elder *Fall of the Rebel Angels* 95
Buraq 101
Burne-Jones, Sir Edward Coley 19, 28, 116, 126, 160, 173, 175, 193
    The Annunciation 44
Burns, Robert *Sir Galahad* 127, 129
Buti, Lucrezia 56
Butts, Thomas 79

C

Cabanel, Alexandre
    Birth of Venus 182
    Expulsion from Paradise 24
Candle in the Dark 123
Caravaggio, Michelangelo Merisi da *Saint Matthew and the Angel* 113
Carolus-Duran 166
Carracci, Annibale
    Annunciation 39
    Paris and Mercury 184
Carroll, Lewis 131, 197
Cézanne, Paul 169, 182
Chaos 157
Chaperone Cyclists' Association 170
cherubim 10, 21, 24, 59, 75, 98, 101, 105, 155
cherubs 39, 55, 59, 70, 118, 152, 155, 191
Christianity 10, 12, 19, 32, 46, 91, 118, 149, 182, 184, 186
Cirera, Jaume *Angels Fighting Devils* 92
Coffin, William Haskell *Share in the Victory* 197
Coleridge, Samuel Taylor *Rime of the Ancient Mariner* 96
Confraternity of Saint Raphael 29
Corbourld, Edward Henry 129
Cortona, Pietro da *The Guardian Angel* 121
Council of Ephesus 32
Council of Trent 39
Counter Reformation 39, 40, 69, 120, 191
Crane, Walter *My Soul Is An Enchanted Boat* 193
Crespi, Giuseppe Maria *The Resurrection of Christ* 80
Cromek, Robert 102
Cronus 187
Crucifixion 72, 75, 77

Cupid 118, 157, 159, 160, 163, 165, 166, 169, 170, 172–73, 175, 177

D

Danhauer, Gottfried *Peter the Great and the Battle of Poltava* 187
Dante *Inferno* 96, 135, 151
David, Jacques-Louis *Cupid and Psyche* 157
De Morgan, Evelyn *An Angel Piping to the Souls in Hell* 151
De Predis Brothers
    An Angel in Green with a Vielle 139
    An Angel in Red with a Lute 139
De Quincey, Thomas *Confessions of an English Opium Eater* 132
Dearle, John Henry *The Passing of Venus* 172–73
Delacroix, Eugène *Triumph of Saint Michael* 91
Dobrynine, Yaroslav and Galina *Saint Michael* 91
Domenico Alfani di Paride *Madonna and Child amongst the Saints Gregory and Nicholas* 63
Doré, Gustave 92
    Fall of the Rebel Angels 96
    O Adam, One Almighty Is, From Whom All Things Proceed 27
Dove 32, 40, 75, 113
Duccio di Buoninsegna *Rucellai Madonna* 56, 77
Dürer, Albrecht 182

E

Egypt 10, 12, 52, 86, 87, 92
    Tomb of Bannantiu 13
El Greco *The Annunciation* 40
Eros 115, 157, 159, 165
Euripides 163

F

Fall of the Rebel Angels 92, 93, 95, 96
Fame 187
Fellowes-Prynne, Edward A. *Ecce Ancilla Domini* 43, 50
Ferrier, Gabriel-Joseph-Marie-Augustin
    L'Ange Gardien 124
    The Love Letter 170
Fetti, Domenico 43
Fetti, Lucrina *The Annunciation* 43
Fiorentino, Rosso *Musical Angel* 145
Fra Angelico
    Angel of the Annunciation 34
    Annunciation 32, 39
    Christ the Judge 109
    Dormition and Assumption of the Virgin 65
    Last Judgement 107
Fra Filippo Lippi *Madonna and Child with Angels* 56
Frampton, Edward Reginald *Saint Catherine* 116

G

Gabriel 19, 32, 39, 40, 43, 44, 46, 50, 52
Gaddi, Taddeo *The Crucifixion* 75
Gainsborough, Thomas 197
Galahad 127, 129, 130

Gaugin, Paul 116
gender 65
Gentileschi, Artemisia 145
Gentileschi, Orazio *Saint Cecilia Playing the Spinet with an Angel* 145
Gérome, Jean-Léon 166
Ghedine, Giuseppe *Assumption of the Virgin* 70
Ghirlandaio, Domenico *Coronation of the Virgin with Saints* 62
Gilbert, Sir Alfred 129
Giotto di Bondone *The Lamentation* 72, 75
Gladstone, William 131
Gloag, Isobel Lilian *Four Corners to My Bed* 123
God the Father 24, 39, 75, 93, 98, 101
Golden Legend 39, 46, 62, 69
Gonzaga, Vincenzo 43
Gospels 46, 54, 79, 82, 85, 107, 110, 113, 120, 124
Graves A. *The Good Fight* 129
Greece 10, 12, 87, 157, 159, 186, 187
    Winged Victory of Samothrace 14
Grimm's Fairy Tales 61
guardian angels 29, 91, 118, 120, 121, 123, 124

H

Hallé, Noël *Venus and Putti* 177
Heaven 98, 104
Hell 92, 93, 98
Herod 52
Hesiod 157
Holy Ghost (Holy Spirit) 32, 40, 46, 50, 75
Holy Grail 118, 126, 127
Horatius Cocles Crowned by Victory 191
hortus conclusus 32, 34, 50
Humanism 75
Hunt, Holman 121

I

Iblis 22
Immaculate Conception 69
In Terris Pax Hominibus Bonae Voluntatis 195
Incarnation 32, 50
Iris 14
Isaac 17, 19
Ishmael 19
Isis 13
Islam 10, 19, 22, 32, 39
    guardian angels 118
Israelites 12, 31

J

Ja'Far al-Sadiq
    Adam and Eve 22
    Ascent of the Prophet to Heaven 101
Jackson, Frederick Hamilton *Lancelot's Vision of the Holy Grail* 127
Jesus Christ 19, 32, 34, 39, 46, 50, 108
    Crucifixion 72, 75, 77
    Infant Jesus 52, 54, 55, 59, 61, 63
    Resurrection 69, 72, 80, 82
Jibril (Jibreel) 19, 39

John the Baptist 39, 43, 110
Joseph 39, 55
Joseph of Arimathea 129
Judaism 10, 31, 32, 39, 44, 152
Judgment 39, 86, 87, 91, 98, 107, 109, 182
Julius II 111, 152
Juno 178, 184
Jupiter 184

K

Ka'aba 39
Kane, H.H. *Drugs That Enslave* 132
Kelmscott Press *Chaucer* 28, 104
Knaus, Ludwig *Peace* 194
Koran 19, 39

L

Lady Day 32, 46
Lalli, A.C.
    *Dante's Dream at the Time of the Death of
    Beatrice* 135
    Why Seek Ye the Living Among the Dead? 85
lamassus 12
Lamb 54, 98
    Van Eyck, Jan and Hubert *The Adoration of
    the Lamb* 79
Lancelot 127
Lattanzio di Niccolò
    Musical Angels with Horn and Zither 143
    Musical Angels with Lute and Violin 140
Léger, Fernand 124
Leonardo da Vinci 29
Liddell, Alice 197
lilies 34, 43, 46, 50, 61, 67
Liss, Johann *The Sacrifice of Isaac* 17
Livy 191
Longinus 72
Lorenzo di Credi *The Annunciation* 37
Low, Will Hicok *Love Disarmed* 166
Lucifer 92
Lutyens, Charles Augustus Henry *Cherubs
    in the Clouds* 155
Lutyens, Edward 155

M

Makowsky, Constantin *The Toilet of Venus* 178
Malory, Sir Thomas *Morte d'Athur* 126
Manet, Edouard 182
Mannerism 187
Mantegna, Andrea *Madonna and Child with
    Cherubs* 59
Margetson, William Henry *The Stranger* 175
Marriott, F. Pickford *The Annunciation* 46
Mars 166
Martino da Udine 75
Mary 19, 32, 34, 37, 39, 40, 43, 44, 45, 46, 49,
    50, 55
    Assumption 62, 65, 67, 69, 70
    Coronation 62, 63, 65
    Immaculate Conception 69
    Madonna and Child 52, 56, 59, 61, 63
Masaccio *The Expulsion from Paradise* 21
Medard, Eugène *L'Amour et Psyche* 163
Memling, Hans *Madonna and Child with Two
    Angels* 59
Mercury 14, 87, 182, 184
Mesopotamia 12, 92

Meteyard, Sidney Harold *Love in Idleness* 177
Michael 86, 87, 88, 91, 93, 95, 98, 182
Michaud *History of the Crusades* 96
Michelangelo 96, 187
Middle Ages 72, 92, 121, 136, 149
Milton, John *Paradise Lost* 27, 92, 95, 96
Minerva 184
Mons, Angel of 124
Moon 69
Moreau, Gustave *Saint Cecilia* 115
Morris, William 44, 126, 173
    Adam and Eve 28, 104
    Angels Welcoming the Saved into Paradise 104
Moses 32, 39
Muhammad 19, 39, 101
Munier, Emile *Le Sauvetage* 166
music 59, 118, 136, 137, 139, 140, 143, 145,
    146–47, 149, 151

N

Nativity 37, 39, 52, 54, 55, 61
Nebuchadnezzar 19
Nephthys 13
New Testament 32, 77
Niccolò da Foligno 140
Nike 14, 118, 191, 197
Noah 39

O

Old Testament 10, 12, 17, 19, 32, 39, 49, 77,
    87, 152
opiates 132
Ovid *Metamorphoses* 163

P

Palmieri, Matteo 67
Pan 159
Paris, Judgment of 184
Paton, Sir Joseph Noël
    *How an Angel Rowed Sir Galahad Across the
    Dern Mere* 130
    Mors Janua Vitae 129
Peace 186, 194, 195
Pears Soap 166
Pellegrino da San Daniele *Crucifixion of Jesus
    Christ* 77
Perrault, Léon Jean Basile
    Cupid's Arrows 163
    Sleeping Angel 155
Persia 10, 19, 22, 91, 92
Perugino, Pietro Vannucci 63, 77, 80
    Eternal Blessing 98
Peter Pan 165
Peter the Great 187
Piero della Francesca *Saint Michael* 86, 88
Pinta, Henri Ludovic Marius
    L'Ange Musicien 149
Pinturicchio *Assumption of the Virgin* 69
Plutarch 191
Poe, Edgar Allan *The Raven* 96
Poussin, Nicolas *The Annunciation* 40
Pozzo, Cassiano dal 40
Pre-Raphaelites 19, 43, 49, 61, 116, 121, 123,
    126, 127, 135, 147, 151, 160, 169, 193
Protestantism 40, 120
Psalms 62, 79, 121
Psyche 157, 163, 165, 170

R

Raimondi, Marcantonio *Mercury* 182
Raphael (archangel) 12, 27, 29, 31, 124
Raphael (artist) 98
    *Crucified Christ with the Virgin Mary, Saints
    and Angels* 77
    Liberation of St Peter 111, 152
    Resurrection of Christ 80
    Sistine Madonna 152
    Virgin and Child 63
Rembrandt van Rijn
    *The Angel Raphael Leaving Tobit and His
    Family* 31
    The Sacrifice of Isaac 17
Renaissance 10, 21, 37, 59, 61, 63, 72, 75, 88,
    98, 140, 143, 157, 178, 186, 187, 189
Reni, Guido
    Coronation of the Virgin 65
    Saint Michael 88
Resurrection 69, 72, 80, 82
Reynolds, Sir Joshua 197
Rhead, George Wooliscroft *O Salutaris Hostia*
    146–47
Rhead, Louis 147
Rococo 177, 191
Romanino, Gaudioso *The Nativity with Saints
    Alexander of Brescia, Jerome, Gaudioso and
    Filippo Benizzi* 55
Rome 12, 14, 19, 87, 111, 113, 184, 186
Rossetti, Dante Gabriel 126, 135, 160
    The Annunciation 43
Rubens, Peter Paul *Saint Sebastian Attended by
    Angels* 113
Rubiev, Andrei *Old Testament Trinity* 14, 17
Ruskin, John 49

S

saints 110, 11, 113, 115, 116
    St Bernard 40, 49
    St Cecilia 115, 145
    St Irene 113
    St Jerome 121
    St Matthew 110
    St Peter 93
    St Sebastian 113
    St Teresa 115
    St Thomas Aquinas 146–47
Samson 43
Santi, Giovanni 77
Sargon II 12
Satan 21, 27, 52, 67, 86, 88
    Fall of the Rebel Angels 92, 95, 96
satyrs 92, 159
Savoldo, Giovanni Girolamo *Tobias and the
    Angel* 29, 31
Savonarola 34
Schiavonetti, Louis 102
Scott, Sir Walter 127, 130
Seignac, Guillaume *The Wings of Desire* 170
seraphim 10, 59, 72, 91, 98, 105, 152
Shaftesbury, Seventh Earl of 165
Shakespeare, William 159
    A Midsummer Night's Dream 149, 177
Shaw, George Bernard 175
shedus 12
Shields, Frederic James *The Light of the
    World* 121

Signorelli, Luca
    Angel and Guitar 137
    The Calling of the Elect into Heaven 109
Sims, Charles *Titania's Awakening* 149
Society for Psychical Research 124, 131
Sodom 32, 39
Solomon, Simeon *Shadrach, Meshach and
    Abednego in the Fiery Furnace* 19
*St Matthew in Bishop More's Book of
    Prayers* 110
Stanhope, John Rodham Spencer 85, 175
    Love and the Maiden 160
Stokes, Adrian 61
Stokes, Marianne *Angels and the Holy Child* 61
Stothard, Thomas *The Expulsion of Adam and
    Eve* 24
Strudwick, John Melhuish *Love and Time* 175
Symbolism 61, 115, 116, 123

T

Talarn, Guillermo *Fall of the Rebel Angels* 93
Tempera Society 61, 116
Tennyson, Alfred, Lord 127, 131, 147
Time 186, 189
Tissot, James
    The Annunciation 45, 102
    The Soul of the Penitent Thief 102
Tobias 12, 29, 31, 121, 124
Trinity 14, 17, 75
    Trinity with Christ Crucified 75
Troy, Jean-François de *Time Unveiling Truth* 189
Truth 189

U

Uranus 182
Urban IV 147

V

Van Eyck, Jan and Hubert
    Adoration of the Lamb 79
    Angels Making Music 137
Van Gogh, Vincent 131
Venus 157, 159, 166, 170, 172–3, 177, 178, 181,
    182, 184
Venusti, Marcello *The Adoration of the
    Shepherds* 54
Victory 14, 118, 191, 197
Virgin and Child *see* Mary: Madonna and Child

W

Wagrez, Jacques-Clément *Eros* 159
Waterhouse, John William *The Annunciation* 49
Watts, G.F. 151
West, Benjamin *Angel of the Lord Announcing the
    Resurrection to the Three Maries at the
    Sepulchre* 82
Whistler, James McNeill 182

Y

Yeats, W.B. 28

Z

Zatzka, Hans *The Birth of Venus* 181
Zenale, Bernadino *Saint Michael* 87